HANDBOOK ON SMALL BORE RIFLE SHOOTING

EQUIPMENT
MARKSMANSHIP
TARGET SHOOTING
PRACTICAL SHOOTING
RIFLE RANGES
RIFLE CLUBS

BY

COLONEL TOWNSEND WHELEN

Copyright © 2013 Read Books Ltd.
This book is copyright and may not be
reproduced or copied in any way without
the express permission of the publisher in writing

British Library Cataloguing-in-Publication Data
A catalogue record for this book is available from the
British Library

CONTENTS

TOWNSEND WHELEN 1

INTRODUCTION 4

CHAPTER I - EQUIPMENT 9

CHAPTER II - MARKSMANSHIP 34

CHAPTER III - AIMING 39

CHAPTER IV - THE FIRING POSITIONS 45

CHAPTER V - TRIGGER SQUEEZE 66

CHAPTER VI - SIGHT ADJUSTMENT AND
RANGE PRACTICE 72

CHAPTER VII - SLOW FIRING 91

CHAPTER VIII - RAPID FIRE 107

CHAPTER IX - TOURNAMENTS AND
COMPETITIONS 113

CHAPTER X - FIELD SHOOTING 121

CHAPTER XI - CARE OF THE RIFLE 128

CHAPTER XII - SMALL BORE TARGETS 135

CHAPTER XIII - SMALL BORE RIFLE RANGES 141

CHAPTER XIV - THE RIFLE CLUB AND THE NATIONAL RIFLE ASSOCIATION 172

Townsend Whelen

Townsend Whelen was born on 6 March 1877. Known as 'Townie' to his friends, Whelen was an American hunter, writer, outdoorsman, rifleman and soldier. He served as a Colonel in the United States army, and was famed for his skill and accuracy with a gun. Whelen could reportedly hit a man-sized target at 200 yards, using the bolt action, open-sighted M1903 Springfield .30-06 service rifle. He was able to score six hits in ten seconds flat, and, perhaps more importantly, could do this on command. He is famous for saying that 'only accurate rifles are interesting' and that 'the .30-06 is never a mistake.' The .30-06 was a cartridge introduced into the U.S. army in 1906, and later standardised; remaining in official use until the early 1970s. Whelen experimented with the service .30-06 Springfield cartridge while he was commanding officer of Frankford Arsenal in the early 1920s. He modified the .30-06 case to fire bullets of different calibers, and was particularly interested in creating a cartridge to fire heavier bullets from M1903 rifle actions.

Aside from his life as a gun-man, Whelen also served as contributing editor to *Sports Afield*, *American Rifleman*, *Field and Stream*, *Outdoor Life*, *Guns and Ammo*, and other magazines – as well as authoring several of his own books; *Telescopic Rifle Sights, The Hunting Rifle, Small Arms and Ballistics, Hunting Big Game,* and *Why Not Load Your Own.* Whelen also attempted to write his own autobiography, but never finished the endeavour. It was entitled *Mr Rifleman,* and was eventually completed by his family, and published posthumously. Whelen died on 23 December 1961 at the age of eighty-four. He created the .25, .35, .375 and .400 Whelen Cartridges.

CAMP PERRY, OHIO

The Mecca of

Small Bore Riflemen

Introduction

THIS handbook is intended for the beginner in rifle shooting. It gives the principles on which good marksmanship is based in a practical manner so that the reader can apply them without an instructor, and thus teach himself to shoot. Without a knowledge of these principles, many delays and difficulties would lie in the path of the beginner.

When the reader has become familiar with and proficient in the basic principles, he should take up target shooting at known distances, wherein he learns to apply these principles—literally to hit where he aims. He thus perfects himself in all the essentials of good shooting. In shooting at bull's-eye targets one can see his errors as well as his good shots, and can thus correct his mistakes.

Then one should graduate to practical shooting wherein he learns to hit more or less indistinct objects, to hit them rapidly, and to shoot at varying distances where the ranges must be estimated. He also learns to hit moving objects.

Following the shooting portion of the handbook, instructions are given for the building of convenient, safe, and economical rifle ranges without which, of course, practice in rifle shooting could not be had. And then the handbook describes the methods of organizing and conducting rifle clubs which are a great aid in promoting interest and sport as they introduce the competitive and co-operative elements.

The handbook confines itself chiefly to small bore shooting, that is shooting with .22 caliber rifles, because such shooting is inexpensive, ranges may be erected anywhere, even indoors, and markers are not necessary at the targets. Small bore shooting teaches all the essentials of good marksmanship so that the shooter qualified at it can graduate to the big rifle and do well with that weapon from the very start, all the principles applying equally to either weapon.

Rifle shooting is a clean, manly, invigorating sport for men and boys, and indeed women and girls are finding that it is attractive and suited to them also. It teaches care, precision, and close attention to little details, all so essential for success in any life undertaking. It improves the health and particularly the eyesight and the co-ordination of the body. It makes for clean, straight living, for one must live straight, and think straight, and be straight to shoot straight. The men and boys whom one finds indulging in rifle shooting are invariably straight mentally, physically, and morally. No God-gifted physique is necessary for success in shooting as is so often essential in other sports. The small, lightly built man, woman, boy or girl has just as good a chance to get to the top as their more sturdy companions. There never has been the slightest taint of professionalism in rifle shooting, and there never will be. It is a clean, manly American sport.

It Is Very Strongly Advised That You Read Chapter II Before Proceeding to the Remainder of the Handbook

NOMENCLATURE OF SMALL BORE TARGET RIFLE

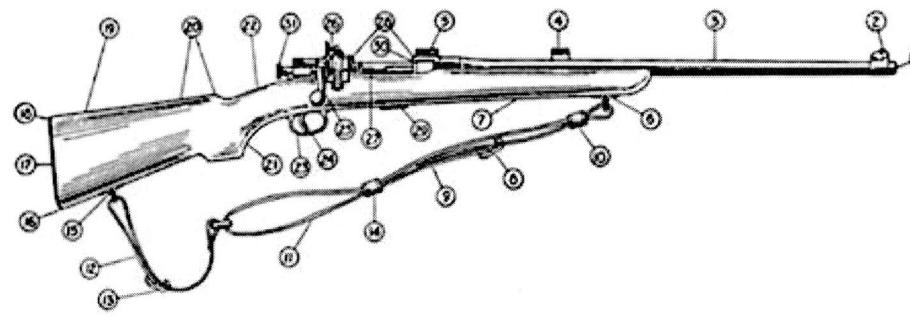

1—Muzzle.

2—Front Sight.

3—Barrel.

4—Front Telescope Block.

5—Rear Telescope Block.

6—Front Sling Swivel.

7—Forearm.

8—Front Claw.

9—Gunsling.

10—Front Keeper.

11—Loop of Gunsling.

12—Tailpiece of Gunsling.

13—Rear Claw.

14—Rear Keeper.

15—Butt Sling Swivel.

16—Toe of Stock.

17—Butt-plate.

18—Heel of Stock.

19—Butt-stock.

20—Comb of Stock.

21—Pistol Grip.

22—Small of Stock.

23—Trigger Guard.

24—Trigger.

25—Bolt Handle.

26—Receiver Sight.

27—Bolt.

28—Receiver.

29—Magazine.

30—Breech.

31—Cocking Piece.

Safety, not shown, near rear of Receiver.

CHAPTER I

EQUIPMENT

The equipment necessary for small bore rifle shooting is neither expensive nor numerous. You will need, of course, a proper rifle and ammunition. A small telescope to spot the shots on the target is very desirable. Then there are a few accessories such as cleaning materials, telescope rest, and cartridge block, many of which can be gotten together quickly. No special clothing is needed. Given these, and a suitable rifle range, which can often be had on a nearby farm, and you are ready to go ahead, using this handbook as a guide.

THE RIFLE

The rifle should be one using the .22 caliber Long Rifle rim fire cartridge. Rifles which are suitable for serious work, and for the development of a high degree of skill in marksmanship, may be divided into two classes: the heavy or match type (*i.e.* 9 pounds or over) which we call Class A rifles, and the medium match type (*i.e.* under 9 pounds) which we call Class B rifles.

Class A Rifles: These include small bore target rifles having adjustable sights, specially designed target stocks, sling straps, and other accessories which make for success in accurate target shooting. These rifles are the choice of our expert shots, and are the class of rifles commonly used in large and important matches. (See Plate 1.)

Winchester Model 52 Bull Gun

Speed lock, bolt action, extra heavy weight 28-inch barrel, Vaver W11A front sight, Vaver 5237 extension rear sight with 1/8 minute clicks, Marksman No. 1 stock, adjustable front sling swivel, telescope bases, weight 13 1/2 pounds.

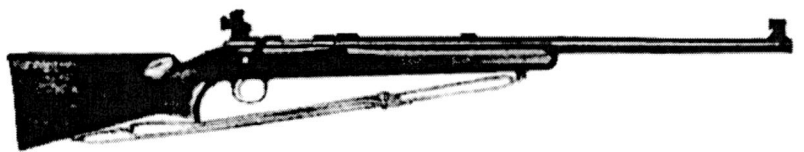

Remington Model 37 "Rangemaster" Target Rifle

Bolt action. 5 shot box magazine, 28-inch heavy barrel, Remington micrometer rear sight adjustable to quarter minutes, globe front sight with seven interchangeable inserts, sling strap with adjustable front swivel, weight about 12 pounds.

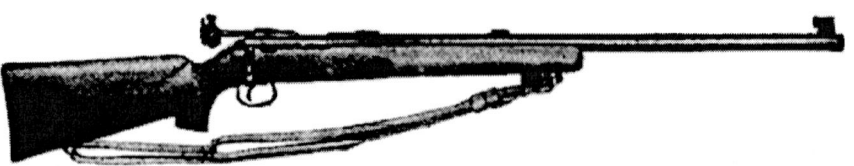

Winchester Model 52 Heavy Barrel Target Rifle

Bolt action, 5 shot magazine, 28-inch heavy barrel, micrometer extension rear sight, adjustable to quarter minutes, quick detachable front sight, Springfield type sling and adjustable sling swivels with hand protector, full beavertail forearm, high comb, weight about 12 pounds.

Handbook on Small Bore Rifle Shooting

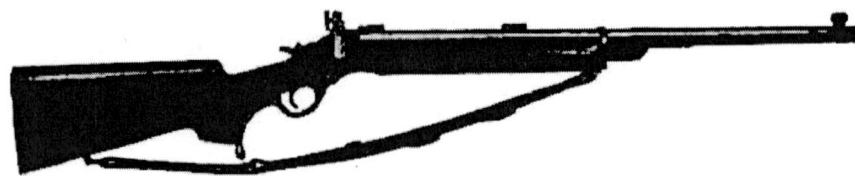

Stevens No. 417-1 Walnut Hill Target Rifle

Single shot, Stevens X-ring. 28-inch heavy target barrel, Stevens "Ideal" breech block, lever action, automatic ejector, complete with Lyman No. 48L rear and Lyman No. 17A front sights, telescope blocks, and leather sling strap, weight 10 1/2 pounds.

Winchester Model 52 Standard Barrel Target Rifle

Bolt action, 5 shot magazine, 28-inch barrel, micrometer rear sight with quarter minute clicks, interchangeable disc front sight, scope blocks, sling swivels, weight about 10 pounds.

Handbook on Small Bore Rifle Shooting

Stevens 416-2 Target Rifle

Repeating, bolt action, 5 shot magazine, Stevens X-ring 26-inch heavy tapered barrel, speed lock, adjustable trigger pull, fitted with Stevens No. 106 rear and Stevens No. 25 hooded front sight, telescope blocks, leather sling strap, weight 9 1/2 pounds.

PLATE 1

Class B Rifles: These are similar to those listed in Class A, except that they are lighter in weight and less expensive.

Remington Model 513TR "Matchmaster" Rifle

Bolt action, 6 shot box magazine, 27-inch barrel, micrometer rear sight, adjustable to quarter minutes, globe front sight with seven interchangeable inserts, sling strap with adjustable front swivel, weight about 9 pounds.

Handbook on Small Bore Rifle Shooting

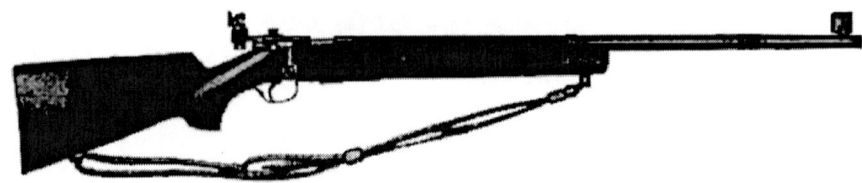

Winchester Model 75 Target Rifle

Bolt action with speed lock, 5 shot magazine, 28-inch tapered barrel, pistol grip stock with semi-beavertail fore-end, high comb, Winchester 99A front sight, Winchester 84A extension rear sight with 1/4-inch clicks for windage and elevation, side lever safety, adjustable sling swivel base, 1 1/4-inch Army type leather sling strap, tan color, weight 8 pounds 10 ounces.

Savage Model 19 Target Rifle

Repeating, bolt action, 5 shot magazine, 25-inch medium weight barrel, speed lock, fitted with No. 15 Savage extension rear sight, hooded front sight, tapped for telescope blocks, leather sling strap, weight

8 pounds. Model 19-M, same specifications as above except heavy target barrel, weight 9 1/4 pounds.

Mossberg Model 44B Target Rifle

Bolt action, 7 shot magazine, 13/16-inch heavy type 26-inch barrel, receiver peep sight adjustable, quick detachable swivels, weight 8 pounds.

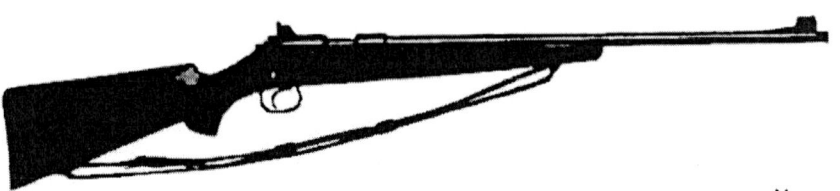

Winchester Model 52 Sporting Rifle

Bolt action, 5 shot magazine, 24-inch barrel, rear sight adjustable to half minutes, sling swivels and sling, weight about 7 1/4 pounds.

Handbook on Small Bore Rifle Shooting

Remington Model 513SA "Sporter" Rifle

Bolt action, 6 shot box magazine, step adjustable sporting rear sight, Patridge type front sight, sporting stock, with grip and fore-end checkered, weight about 6 3/4 pounds.

Winchester Model 75 Sporting Rifle

Bolt action, 5 shot magazine, 24-inch tapered barrel with forged ramp front sight base and sight cover, sporting type pistol grip, American walnut stock with fore-end and pistol grip checkered, pistol grip cap, Lyman 57E receiver sight, post front sight with sight cover, 1-inch swivel bows attached, weight 6 1/2 pounds.

PLATE 2

Class C Rifles: Plate 2A shows a number of rifles of a lower price type than those shown in Class B. They are suitable for general and short range target shooting. These rifles will be found satisfactory for beginners and for those desiring target shooting at low cost.

REPEATING MODELS

Savage Model 4-S Repeating Rifle

Bolt action, 5 shot magazine, 24-inch barrel, rear peep sight, with elevation and windage adjustments and sighting disc with three sizes of apertures, hooded front sight with three inserts, weight 5 1/2 pounds.

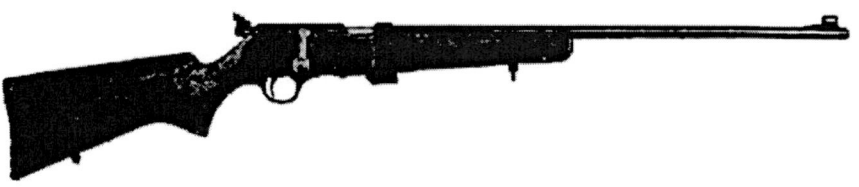

Marlin Model 80-DL Repeating Rifle

Bolt action, 8 shots, clip magazine, 24-inch round barrel, peep sight, ramp front sight and hood, swivels, weight about 6 pounds.

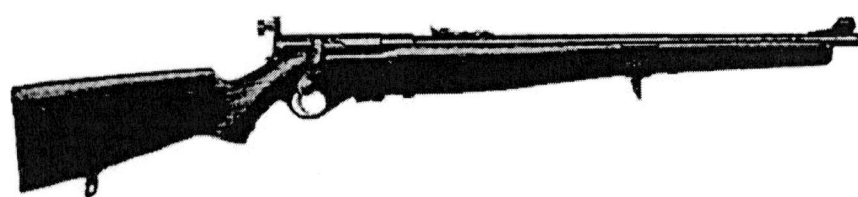

Mossberg Model 42M Rifle

Bolt action, 7 shot magazine, 23-inch barrel, receiver peep sight, quick detachable swivels, weight 6 3/4 pounds.

Mossberg Model 42D Rifle

Bolt action, 7 shot clip magazine, 24-inch barrel, receiver peep sight, swivels, weight 5 1/2 pounds.

Remington Model 511P "Scoremaster" Repeating Rifle

Bolt action, 6 shot box magazine, 25-inch barrel, receiver peep sight with two interchangeable discs, blade front sight, weight about 5 3/4 pounds.

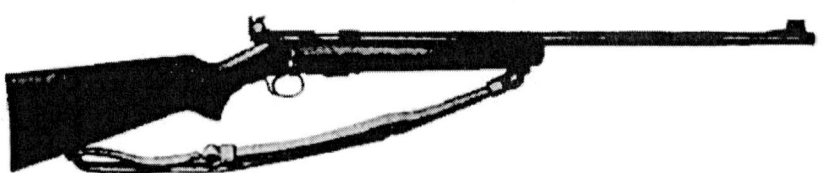

Winchester Model 6941

Bolt action, single shot adapter or 5 shot magazine optional, 25-inch round tapered barrel, American walnut stock, pistol grip, semi-beavertail fore-end, fitted with Lyman 57E receiver sight and Winchester 101 post front sight, 1-inch Army type leather sling strap, weight 6 pounds.

Winchester Model 6940

Bolt action, single shot adapter or 5 shot magazine optional, 25-inch round tapered barrel. American walnut stock, pistol grip, semi-beavertail fore-end, fitted with 80A rear peep sight and Winchester 93 post front sight, no cover, 1-inch Army type leather sling strap, weight 6 pounds.

Stevens No. 056 Repeating Rifle

Bolt action, 5 shot magazine, 24-inch barrel, rear peep sight, with elevation and windage adjustments and sighting disc with three sizes of apertures, hooded front sight with three inserts, weight 5 1/2 pounds.

SINGLE SHOT MODELS

Mossberg Model 26B Rifle

Bolt action, single shot, 26-inch barrel, receiver peep sight, sling swivels, weight 5 1/2 pounds.

Marlin Model 101-DL Rifle

Bolt action, single shot, self-cocking, 24-inch round barrel, weight about 5 pounds.

Savage Model 3-S Rifle

Bolt action, single shot, 26-inch barrel, rear peep sight with elevation and windage adjustments and sighting disc with three sizes of apertures, hooded front sight with three inserts, weight 4 1/2 pounds.

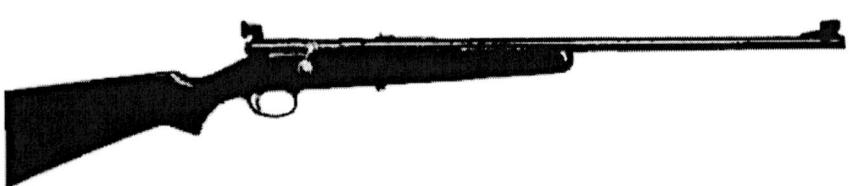

Stevens No. 053 Rifle

Bolt action, single shot, 26-inch barrel, rear peep sight with elevation and windage adjustments and sighting disc with three sizes of apertures, hooded front sight with three inserts, weight 4 1/2 pounds.

Remington Model 510P "Targetmaster" Rifle

Bolt action, single shot, 25-inch barrel, receiver peep sight with two interchangeable discs, blade front sight, weight about 5 3/4 pounds.

Handbook on Small Bore Rifle Shooting

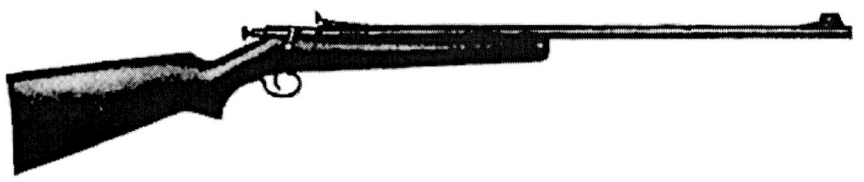

Winchester Model 68

Bolt action, 27-inch round tapered barrel ground at the muzzle, military type safety lock, American walnut sporting type pistol grip stock and semi-beavertail fore-end, Winchester 97A bead front sight or Winchester 101 front sight optional, Winchester 96A rear peep sight, adjustable for windage and elevation, weight 5 1/2 pounds.

PLATE 2A

Most of the makers of these rifles will be found listed in this handbook. If you are interested in any particular rifle you can see it at the nearest dealers, or you can write to the manufacturer for a descriptive circular of it. Other .22 caliber rifles, usually of light weight, not fitted with adjustable aperture sights or slings, are intended for special purposes. In general no very fine shooting, or the development and maintenance of interest and skill in marksmanship, can be expected from these rifles outside of their special lines of usefulness.

THE CARTRIDGE

The cartridge to use, and for which the foregoing rifles are adapted, is that known as the .22 Long Rifle cartridge shown in Plate 3. Many varieties of this cartridge are made by the various cartridge manufacturers. They may be divided roughly into three classifications: First, those intended for top-notch competitive match shooting. Second, those intended for target shooting, practice firing and hunting. Third, those designed for game, vermin shooting and plinking.

PLATE 3

The cartridges in the first two classes are loaded to muzzle velocities between 1,070 and 1,200 feet per second and are available with smokeless or Lesmok powder, lubricated bullets and non-corrosive priming mixture. These are the most desirable for target shooting and have been used successfully up to 300 yards. However, the principal matches at this time are not beyond 200 yards.

The cartridges in the third class are loaded to approximately 1,400 feet per second muzzle velocity, and are intended for shooting at unknown ranges where their flatter trajectory minimizes the small errors of estimating distances. They also have increased shocking power which is of the utmost importance in small game and vermin shooting, and can be obtained with regular lead, plated or coated, and hollow point bullets. While these cartridges are surprisingly accurate at all practical hunting ranges, as a general rule they will not give quite as good performances for fine target shooting as the special target and match cartridges.

Double Target Frames. See page 69

The same .22 Long Rifle cartridge will shoot with practically the same velocity in any standard rifle. The extreme range, with barrel elevated at an angle of about 30 degrees, is about 1,400 yards for the target and match cartridges and about 1,600 yards for the high velocity cartridges having a muzzle velocity of approximately 1,400 feet per second, and the bullets are capable of doing damage at these extreme ranges.

Rifles of the classes listed above should be fired only with the .22 Long Rifle cartridge. The cartridge known as the .22 Short cannot give its best performance in rifles chambered for the .22 Long Rifle cartridges and at the same time its prolonged use is detrimental to fine barrels.

On page 12 are listed the various cartridges as manufactured by the different loading companies. They are classified according to the foregoing and include the trade names of the respective brands. Unless otherwise specified, all are smokeless loads.

ACCESSORIES

Perhaps the most essential accessory for small bore rifle shooting is a spotting telescope. This you place alongside of you as you shoot, resting it on a small stand which holds the scope trained and focused on the target, and about a foot above the ground. After you shoot, you look through the telescope and you see where the bullet struck the target. Thus if you are shooting alone it is not necessary for you to get out of position and go down to the targets until all have been fired on. Nor is it necessary to have markers at the target, and this very considerably cheapens range construction and operation.

Not all telescopes will show a bullet hole in the target at 100 yards, and very few will do so at 200 yards. Usually at 200 yards we have to depend on markers at the butt to indicate the position of our shots to us with spotters. For use up to and including 100 yards the telescope, generally speaking, should have a magnifying power of at least 20 diameters, together with a very large object lens. Resolving power is not a matter of magnification alone, but also depends largely upon the diameter of the object lens. Very powerful telescopes, unless they are accompanied with very large object lenses, are not desirable, and then they are very expensive.

CLASSIFICATION OF .22 LONG RIFLE CARTRIDGES

BRAND, TRADE NAME AND TYPE BULLET

Match Cartridges	Target, Practice and Hunting Cartridges	High Velocity Game and Vermin Cartridges
FEDERAL			
	Monark Smokeless, Non-Corrosive, Lead Bullet, Lubricated	Hi-Power Excess Speed, Non-Corrosive, Lead Bullet, Lubricated Hi-Power Excess Speed, Non-Corrosive, Hollow Point, Lead Bullet, Lubricated
PETERS			
2296—"Dewar" Match, Rustless, Lead Lubricated Bullet 2223—"Police Match," Rustless, Lead Lubricated Bullet	2224—"Target," Rustless, Lead Lubricated Bullet	2283—High Velocity, Rustless, Lead Lubricated Bullet 2284—High Velocity, Rustless, Hollow Point, Lead Lubricated Bullet

REMINGTON

R54P — Palma Kleanbore, Lead Lubricated Bullet R22T—Police Targetmaster, Kleanbore, Lead Lubricated Bullet	R19—New and Improved Kleanbore, Lead Lubricated Bullet R17L — Regular Kleanbore, Lead Bullet	R21—Hi-Speed, Kleanbore, Lead Lubricated Bullet R23—Hi-Speed, Kleanbore, Hollow Point, Lead Lubricated Bullet

WESTERN

K1228R—Super Match, Non-Corrosive, Lubricated Lead Bullet K1267R—Super Match Mark II, Non-Corrosive, Lubricated Lead Bullet	K1264R—Xpert, Non-Corrosive, Lubricated Lead Bullet	K1225R — Super-X, Non-Corrosive, Lubaloy Coated Bullet, Waxed K1226R — Super-X, Non-Corrosive, Lubaloy Coated Hollow Point Bullet, Waxed

WINCHESTER

K2238R — Precision EZXS, Lubricated Lead Bullet (Lesmok)	K2340R—All-X Match Staynless, Lubricated Lead Bullet K2388R — Leader Staynless, Lubricated Lead Bullet	K2208R—Super Speed Staynless, Kopperklad Solid Bullet, Wax Coated K2207R—Super Speed Staynless, Kopperklad Hollow Point Bullet, Wax Coated

NOTE:—In every case above, the words ".22 Long Rifle" should precede the trade name as above. Do not confuse ".22 Long Rifle" cartridges with ".22 Long," ".22 Short," ".22 W.R.F.," ".22 Special," ".22 Automatic," or ".22 Extra Long" cartridges, all of these last cartridges being entirely different cartridges from the ".22 Long Rifle" cartridges described above.

Correct as of April 1, 1941.

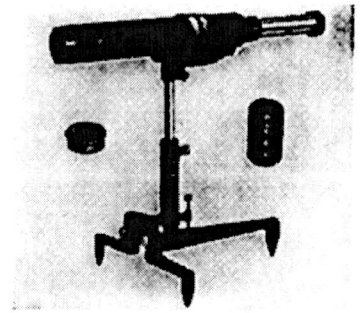

PLATE 4A—Spotting Telescopes

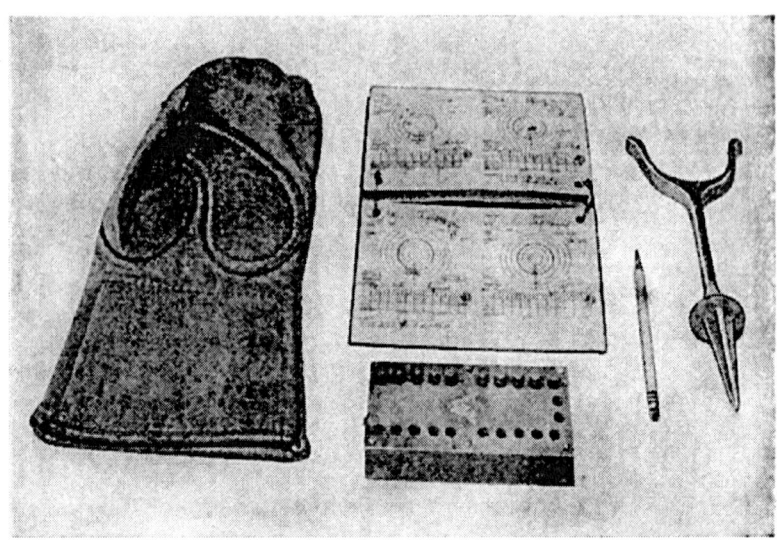

PLATE 4B—Desirable Accessories—Shooting Glove, Score Book, Pencil, Forked Rifle Rest and Cartridge Block

Other worth-while accessories are a forked rifle rest to hold the rifle between shots when shooting prone, thus relieving the arms of its tiring weight, and a cartridge block. These can be purchased from any dealer in shooters' supplies and are not expensive. The cartridge block is a little square of wood with holes bored in it in which you place your cartridges. If the match calls for 10 or 20 shots you place just that number in the block, and feed them from the block into the rifle. Thus you are relieved of the necessity of counting, and you shoot just the correct number of shots.

Targets may be secured from licensed manufacturers of official National Rifle Association targets or from their distributors, or from dealers in riflemen's supplies. They are printed on good paper, the correct and official size for shooting at 50 and 75 feet indoors, and 50, 100, and 200 yards outdoors, such as are used in all recognized small bore shooting in this country and England. You simply tack them on the target butt, or on the rack which is hung on the butt.

The only other accessories you need are those for the proper cleaning and care of the rifle—a good cleaning rod, cut flannel patches, and a can of gun oil. A padded shooting coat is desirable. Any loose fitting coat that does not bind across the shoulders will do. The elbows should be padded for comfort when shooting prone. sheepskin with the fleece on it making the best padding material.

PLATE 4C—Showing padded shooting coat, shooting glasses, and kit box

Very efficient telescope sights are now made, suitable for use on small bore rifles. These will be found particularly desirable for those with defective vision, and many small bore matches permit their use. Their manufacturers will send completely descriptive circulars on request.

The Sporting Arms and Ammunition Manufacturers' Institute, 103 Park Avenue, New York, N. Y., has prepared an up-to-date list of the manufacturers of arms, ammunition, targets, equipment, accessories and supplies useful or necessary for small bore rifle shooting. This list will be mailed free by the Institute to all requesting the same. It will tell you just where to obtain everything that you need. Please print your name and address legibly.

CHAPTER II

MARKSMANSHIP

A good shot is never born such, although he may inherit that perfect co-ordination of brain, eye, nerve, and muscle which will make it easy for him to excel in shooting if he is started right. But good shooting is possible with every person who has a fairly good physique, good habits, and good eyesight, either with or without glasses. The trouble is that many people start wrong in shooting a rifle, and they learn bad habits which they then have to break if they are ever to shoot well; particularly they learn bad habits as to trigger squeeze. It seems to be instinctive to jerk the trigger, which is fatal to good shooting. The fine rifle shot is not a man with iron nerves and keen eyesight as popularly supposed; but rather, if it can be described in a few words, he is a man who has learned how to squeeze the trigger.

There are three primary essentials in rifle shooting which must be thoroughly learned before one can even start on the road toward good shooting. These are *aiming, holding,* and *trigger squeeze,* and the most important of these is *trigger squeeze.* These three essentials must be learned together as their co-ordination plays an important part. If one aims his rifle accurately, if he holds it steadily, and then if he squeezes the trigger so as not to spoil the aim and hold, he will always strike the bull—provided his rifle and ammunition are accurate and his sights are correctly adjusted. Here is where co-ordination comes in, that is the teamwork between eye, brain, and muscle to hold the rifle and send the bullet on its way.

In addition to these primary essentials, the beginner should learn the mechanical operation of his rifle, how to adjust the sights, how to allow for wind, and how to take care of his weapon. This is really all there is to rifle shooting, and once the beginner has mastered these things he becomes a good shot, and soon progresses to an excellent shot. Real expertness, as in every other sport, requires experience that comes only with much practice and time.

The bugbear of the beginner is inability to hold the rifle steadily. Using the usual antiquated methods, it takes a very long time, and tedious and often discouraging practice to learn to hold the rifle steadily. Before the average shooter becomes proficient in holding by these old and obsolete methods, he is usually completely discouraged, loses all interest, and quits the game. Until he can hold steadily he cannot see if he is aiming right or not, and likewise he cannot apply the correct trigger squeeze. Prior to the development of our present system of shooting, and instruction in shooting, not one beginner in a thousand developed into a good rifle shot.

But in about five days' practice of half an hour a day, a beginner, following the instructions which follow, can teach himself to hold the rifle almost absolutely steady IN THE PRONE POSITION WITH THE GUNSLING. *In this position, not being bothered with holding difficulties, he can apply himself to accurate aiming, to proper control of the trigger, and to their co-ordination. Then, having learned to make a small group of shots anywhere on the target, he can teach himself sight adjustment, learning to move this group promptly into the center of the bull's-eye. Thus he learns to hit small objects. Therefore the beginner should always* START SHOOTING IN THE PRONE POSITION WITH THE GUNSLING, *and should perfect his holding, aiming, trigger squeeze, and sight adjustment in this position before he proceeds further. Learn to shoot well prone with the gunsling before taking up other positions.*

Then one should take up the sitting position with the gunsling, which will be found to be but little more difficult than the prone position. Success is thus attained from almost the start.

Shooting in the standing or off-hand position takes much longer to learn before one can become really proficient at it. But the advantage of learning with the .22 caliber rifle is that ammunition is so inexpensive that one can afford that large amount of careful practice that is necessary to become a good off-hand shot.

It will thus be seen that it is necessary that one's rifle be provided with a shooting gunsling. It is also essential that it be equipped with an aperture rear sight that has ready, accurate, and recordable adjustments for both elevation and windage, preferably reading to half minutes. As will be seen later, good rifle shooting is almost a continuous process of sight adjustment, and if one would shoot accurately he must be able to adjust his sights accurately. No good shooting can be done day in and day out, nor can any great interest in the game be sustained with cheap, poorly equipped rifles.

The purpose of the next few chapters is to start the reader right in what has been found to be "the one best way", so that he will progress steadily, and will not develop those bad habits which might limit his ultimate perfection in the art of shooting.

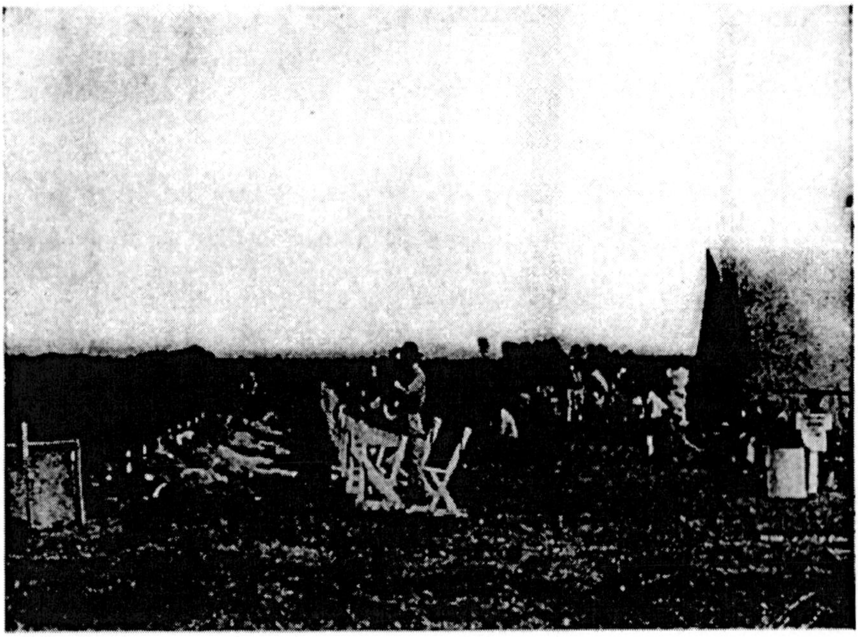

CHAPTER III

AIMING

The greatest pains and precision must be taken about the aim, because any inaccuracy in aiming results in the bullets hitting wide of the mark. A rifle is aimed by first getting the front and rear sights into correct alinement, and then holding them thus alined, moving or directing the rifle so that this line of aim is brought into line with the bull's-eye or other object to be struck.

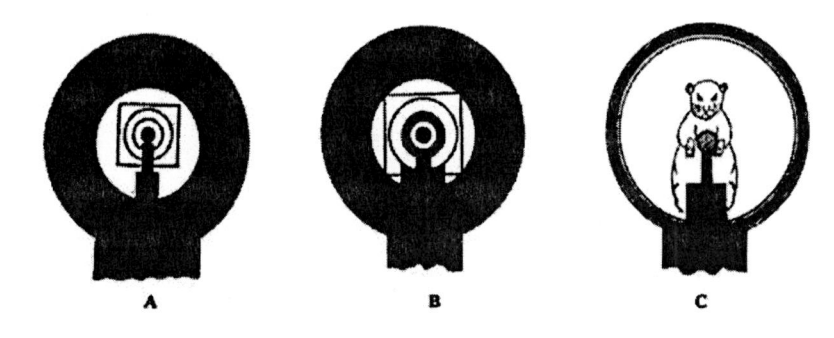

A **B** **C**

PLATE 5

Plate 5 shows how to aim with the various forms of front sights and aperture or peep rear sights. Cut A shows the manner of alining the sights and bull's-eye when the cup disc is used in the rear sight, and when a flat top post front sight is used. This is the usual combination of target sights, and the best for general shooting. The top of the front sight is alined in the center of the peep hole in the disc, and then the rifle is directed at the target so that the top of the front sight appears to almost touch the bottom of the bull's-eye. Both sights are dead black in color, the front sight being kept so by smoking it in the flame of burning camphor or candle. The reason why we aline the front sight below the bull's-eye is to have it appear as a black silhouette against the white surface of the target, so that its exact position is seen distinctly. If we were to attempt to aim at the center of the bull's-eye the black front sight would blend with the black bull's-eye, and you could not tell if you were aiming at the center, top, or bottom of the bull. When using this form of front sight the sights are adjusted so that when aiming at the bottom of the bull, the bullets will strike in the center of the bull's-eye.

You should use the right eye only to aim with, partially closing the left eye. If the right eye is the master eye you may be able to keep both eyes open when aiming, and this may be a slight advantage in giving you clearer vision. Always focus your eye so as to get the best combination vision of the front sight and target. Do not focus on, or look at the rear peep sight, but look through it, letting it blur all it wants to, and center the top of the front sight in this round blur.

Take particular pains to aim precisely the same every time you fire. That is, always try to aline the two sights exactly the same every time, and direct this alinement at the same point below the bull's-eye. Gradually your eye will form a memory "picture" of the sights and target correctly alined, and you will be able to reproduce this picture with great accuracy every time you aim. If the bullet does not strike the bull's-eye when you aim this way, then the sights should be adjusted. You should never aim high or low, or to one side or the other in order to strike the bull's-eye in target shooting. To do so would mean inaccurate aim, because you would not be reproducing the "picture," but would be estimating how much to aim off in a given direction, and we do not want any "estimation" in our aiming.

In all aiming it is *absolutely necessary* that you lay your right cheek firmly against the left side of the comb of the butt-stock in such a position that the eye comes naturally and accurately into the correct line of aim. The firing positions illustrated in Chapter IV show the cheek thus pressed against the stock. This position of the cheek against the comb will be learned quickly and should be assumed the same each time. Only thus can you hold your eye steady in the line of aim and see the sights alined with precision. If your eye were unsupported, and not as if it were a part of the rifle, then the eye would tremble and "bob" around with respect to the rifle, and you could never see the two sights and bull's-eye alined alike for more than a very small instant of time. For this reason, for accurate aim, you should use a rifle having a modern stock with a rather high, thick comb. All of the Class A and B rifles described in Chapter I have such stocks.

For bull's-eye shooting only, if you have keen eyesight, you will gain a slight advantage by using the hooded aperture type of front sight, which is like a little peep sight with a cover or hood to keep it always in the shade and consequently always lighted the same. Cut B shows the manner of alining this type of front sight on the target. The aperture front sight is made to "ring" the bull's-eye, the bull's-eye appearing in its center, and of course the front sight is alined in the middle of the peep rear sight as before. If the bull's-eye does not appear distinct and black through the aperture of the front sight it indicates that either the aperture is too small, or else your eyesight is not quite equal to the task. Hooded aperture sights are provided with a number of aperture discs having various sizes of apertures, and considerable experiment is necessary to find the particular disc which will give the clearest aim with the particular diameter of bull's-eye you are shooting at.

Most modern rear sights have two apertures. There is a type of aperture with large peep and small disc which is a permanent part of the sight, and in addition there is provided a large cup disc with small aperture which may be screwed into the peep-hole. This large disc with small peep is intended only for bull's-eye target shooting, and is best for such shooting. It may sometimes be used for other slow fire shooting where the light is very good and the target well defined, but it is very slow to catch aim with in snap shooting or rapid fire. The large aperture should always be used for all firing at natural targets, for hunting, for rapid fire or snap shooting, and for field shooting. This aperture is usually used in conjunction with a gold, ivory, or red bead front sight. Cut C shows how to aim with such a combination of sights on game. Center the top of the front sight in the center of the aperture, and aline the top of the front sight on the exact spot on the target that you wish your bullet to hit. Focus your eye on target and front sight, look through the rear sight, letting it blur all it wants to, and center the blur. Do not object to the fact that you can see a great deal of country through this large peep-hole, as this is what enables you to catch aim so quickly with this type of rear peep, and to keep moving or running objects continually in view. Take great pains in aiming very accurately in this way for the first week or two, until your eye forms an indelible memory of the picture. Then begin to disregard the rear sight entirely when aiming, merely looking through it but paying no attention to it, letting the eye center the front sight in the peep naturally. This it will do after you have aimed enough carefully to get the "picture" firmly impressed, because the eye has a natural aptitude for centering objects. It is when this method of aiming with the front sight only is learned that the peep-sight becomes the most accurate and rapid of all iron rear sights.

Bright bead sights are not nearly as good as dead black front sights for target shooting, but for all shooting at natural objects or game they are much better because they show up more distinctly against natural backgrounds. Ivory beads are best for deep woods, but are not good over snow. Gold beads are strongest, and can be smoked black for target shooting without injuring them. The surface of the bead toward the eye should always be flat and perpendicular, never rounded. It will then be illuminated evenly all over by sunlight, and the aim will be constant. If the bead were rounded toward the eye, only that portion toward the sun would be illuminated, you would favor that bright spot in aiming, particularly when aiming quickly, and your bullet would strike wide of the mark in the direction away from the sun or light.

Remember to aim exactly the same each time. If your rifle does not shoot where you aim it, then your sights should be adjusted—never alter the method of aiming.

CHAPTER IV

THE FIRING POSITIONS

If you are a beginner in rifle shooting your greatest difficulty at the start will be to hold the rifle steady. In fact for the first three or four days you will not be able to hold steadily enough to aim accurately or to squeeze the trigger properly. You should not attempt to do any shooting at this stage, because you will get no results at all, you would simply waste time and ammunition, and you would become discouraged.

It will take you quite a long time to learn to hold fairly steadily in the standing and kneeling positions, and you should never attempt to shoot in those positions until you have become a really good shot in the prone and sitting positions. Particularly we want you to start to shoot in the prone position with gunsling only. The proper way to learn this position is to practice it first in your home, without cartridges, until you become perfect, steady, and comfortable in it. Not until then should you take your rifle out to the range to do any shooting. In just a few days of practice in this position you can hold the rifle with absolute steadiness, and then you will be able to concentrate on aiming accurately, and squeezing the trigger carefully, a thing you absolutely could not do while your rifle was wobbling all over the landscape.

Practice the prone position in your home for ten minutes, twice a day, until you learn it. Then, when you have become a good shot in this position, similarly practice each of the other positions at home for a few days until you learn them before you start shooting in them. These are the positions used by every rifle shot who has had any success whatsoever.

ADJUSTING THE GUNSLING

The gunsling is of tremendous assistance to steady holding in the prone, sitting, and kneeling positions. We do not mean to say that you cannot shoot in these positions without the gunsling, but we do say that it will take you weeks and months to hold and shoot fairly well without it, and with it you can learn to hold steadily and shoot very well in just a few days. Every expert rifleman uses the gunsling in these positions. Without it he would be hopelessly handicapped when competing against those who use it. But it must be used correctly to get the benefit from it.

PLATE 6—Putting the arm through the loop

The upper or forward half of the sling is called the "loop." When you stretch the sling along the bottom of the stock the loop should be adjusted to such a length that it will come to within about 2 inches of the butt-swivel. Exact length will differ with different lengths of arms, and can only be told from experience. If the loop is too short you cannot get the rifle to your shoulder; if too loose the sling will not be tight on the arm. The rear portion of the sling is called the "tail," and it should always be so loose that it will never be stretched tight when you are in the firing position.

PLATE 7—Left hand, arm, and loop in proper position

To place the sling on your arm, move the hand between the entire sling and the stock just in front of the trigger guard, and then bring the hand and arm back through the loop. That is, your arm should pass through the loop from its right to its left. This twists the upper portion of the sling so that its flat rests against your wrist. See Plate 6. The left hand is then carried in a circular motion, high and left, over the forward part of the sling, and grasps the forearm just in rear of the front sling swivel. With the right hand then pull the loop as high up on the left upper arm as it will go, and slip down the keeper to hold it there, as shown in Plate 7. Notice that the loop passes from the forearm swivel, to the right of the left wrist, and then around the left upper arm high up near the arm pit. The faults of the beginner are placing the hand through the loop from left to right instead of right to left so that the edge instead of flat of sling rests against the right side of the left wrist, and having the rear of the loop around the upper arm near the elbow instead of high up almost to the arm pit.

THE PRONE POSITION

To assume the prone position, having adjusted the sling on the arm as described above, you should first half face to the right of the target, then lie down on your stomach, elbows on the ground, taking particular care that you lie at an angle of 45 degrees to the right of the target, never head on to the target. Place the butt of the rifle to your shoulder and aim at the target. If you cannot get the butt of the rifle to your shoulder the sling is too tight. When the sling is just the right length it takes a little effort, but not much, to place the butt to the shoulder. The left elbow must be on the ground at a point almost under, never more than an inch or two to the left of the rifle. The right elbow should be sloped outward more. The elbows should not be too far apart nor too close together. Regard the upper arms and the chest as the legs of a tripod; if the legs are set too far apart the tripod will be unsteady; also if they are too close together. The forearm should now rest well down in the palm of the hand, fingers curling up over the forearm and fingers and thumb almost but not quite meeting over the top of the barrel. Do not grasp the forearm with the fingers and hold palm away from the bottom of the forearm, but let that forearm press down hard well into the palm of the hand. The sling loop should now be quite tight, binding the forearm down hard in the palm of the hand, and binding the butt quite tight against the shoulder. The sling loop should feel as though it had about 10 to 15 pounds' tension on it.

The legs should be spread wide apart and should hug the ground closely, feet turned outward, and inside of shoes resting on the ground.

Now read all these instructions over again to see that you have gotten them right. Every word is important. Also very carefully study Plates 8, 9 and 20, which show the details of the prone position. Copy them as nearly as you can. At the beginning, this position will probably be intensely uncomfortable. Persist in it. Practice it ten minutes at a time. Try first to get it precisely right. About the third day it will begin to seem more natural and comfortable. The fourth day you will find that you are beginning to hold quite steady. Before the week is out you will find that you can place the sights on the target and hold them alined there steadily.

The principal faults of the beginner are: lying head on to the target instead of faced 45 degrees to the right; left elbow too far to the left of a point directly under the rifle; forearm of rifle not well down in the palm of the hand; sling loop too loose or too tight; and loop around arm down near the elbow instead of high up near arm pit.

PLATE 8—Prone position, right side view

It is well to have some kind of soft padding on the elbows of your shooting coat, otherwise they may get sore from contact with the ground.

HOLDING THE BREATH

When you have gotten the position correctly, and have

practiced it enough so that it is no longer uncomfortable and you are beginning to hold steadily, then you can begin to practice aiming at a small target while attempting to hold steady. When you aim you must hold your breath. Take a deep breath, then let it out until the lungs become normal, and then start to aim. Hold the breath while aiming, and then attempt to squeeze the trigger exactly as described in the next chapter. If it becomes difficult, or you become shaky, bring the rifle down, rest a minute, then try again.

PLATE 9—Prone position, left side view

SITTING POSITION

Do not practice this position until you have become a good shot in the prone position. Adjust the gunsling as before. The sling, arms, hands, and rifle are in the same relative position as when shooting prone. Half face to the right of the target and sit down. Rest the elbows on the knees, or just a little bit below the knees, the left elbow and left knee almost under the rifle. If possible stamp small holes in the ground for the heels to rest in to keep them from slipping. It is also permissible to cross the legs below the knees if you desire and if it gives added steadiness. Gradually you will find that there is just one spot on the knee-caps, or slightly below them, where the elbows will tend to rest firmly. See Plates 10 and 11 and imitate them as closely as possible.

As before, practice this position, and holding, aiming, and squeezing the trigger in it for several days at home, before attempting to use it on the range.

PLATE 10—Sitting position, right side

PLATE 11—Sitting position

THE KNEELING POSITION

Do not practice this position until you have become a good shot in the prone and sitting positions. Adjust the gunsling on the left arm as before. Half face to the right of the target. Sit on the right heel, resting the weight of the body on it. If your ankle is limber enough you may sit on the side of the foot instead of on the heel. The left knee should point toward the target, with the left elbow resting on or a trifle in front of the knee-cap. The sling, hands, arms, and the rifle are in the same relative position as when shooting prone, except the right elbow is not rested. The left elbow should be a little more under the rifle than in the preceding positions. Lean a little forward to get a good balance, then train yourself to control the slight tendency to sway from side to side. See plates 12 and 13, and endeavor to duplicate the position shown as closely as possible.

THE STANDING POSITION

Do not practice this position until you have become a good shot in the prone and sitting positions. After that it should be practiced at home almost daily, and on the range whenever you can do so. It is much more difficult to shoot well standing than in the other positions, and it takes longer to learn it. But as in practical shooting you often cannot assume other positions because there is no time, or because ground or vegetation interfere with a view of the target from lower positions, you should endeavor to perfect yourself in shooting standing. No one is a finished rifleman until he can shoot at least fairly well in the standing position in both slow and rapid fire.

PLATE 12—Kneeling position, right side

PLATE 13—Kneeling position, left side

Face almost directly to the right of the target. The left side should be toward the target, feet from 12 to 18 inches apart as seems steadiest. The left elbow should be well under the rifle. With long-armed shooters the left hand should grasp the forearm well out toward its tip. Short-armed shooters will have to grasp slightly closer to the trigger guard. The right elbow may be held high or low as seems steadiest. Hold the rifle medium hard to the shoulder with the right hand, using the left hand mostly to direct and steady the rifle. The right cheek should be pressed hard against the left side of the buttstock. Let the forearm rest well down in the palm of the hand. Slight variations in this position are permissible, and after considerable experience you may find that you can vary the position with advantage, but at the start you should endeavor to duplicate the position as shown in plates 14 and 15 as closely as possible.

PLATE 14—Army standing position, right side

PLATE 15—Army standing position, left side

It is important that you get a good balance on both feet and the hips. If your body is out of balance you will sway and tremble. Assume an erect, well-balanced standing position without the rifle in the hands. Now when you take up the rifle and aim with it, the weight of the rifle stretched out in front will tend to pull you forward. You should now lean back just a trifle, perhaps an inch or two, just enough to counteract the tendency of the rifle to pull you forward, thus getting in perfect balance. Do not lean forward at all as the beginner and the poor shot usually do.

PLATE 16A—N. R. A. standing position, right side

PLATE 16B—N. R. A. standing position, left side

It takes a lot of practice to learn to hold steadily and shoot well standing. You should practice it daily in your room, assuming the position, aiming most carefully, and then practicing the trigger squeeze, all at a little target on the wall. Every good offhand shot practices daily in this way the whole year, besides getting all the regular shooting on the rifle range that he can find time for.

The position described is known as the "Army Standing" position, and is prescribed in military matches and many matches in R. O. T. C. Units. In N. R. A. Club competitions, the "N. R. A. Standing" position may be used in which it is permissible to use the gunsling, and the elbow of the arm supporting the rifle may be placed against the body or rested on the hip.*

The gunsling is of little or no advantage in standing positions, but often the resting of the left upper arm against the body, or wedging the left elbow into the hip, does give a slightly steadier position, although the "N. R. A. Standing" position is not a quickly assumed one for rapid fire or snap shooting.

For slow fire shooting the position that one finally assumes as his best position will depend much upon his physical conformation. The beginner should experiment a little with slight changes in position before selecting one in which to perfect himself. As one aims and endeavors to hold steadily, the sights will drift and tremble around the bull. It is never possible to hold with such absolute steadiness in the standing position as one can in the prone position, or as often can be done in the sitting position. But with considerable practice one does hold steadier, and he must try to control and time his trigger squeeze so that the last ounce of pressure which discharges the rifle is squeezed or "wished" on just as the front sight drifts under the bull.

Plates 16A and 16B show the standing position which is permitted in Schuetzen, International, and Free Rifle shooting. Note that most of the weight of the body rests on the left leg, and that the left hip is thrust forward to form a shelf on which to rest the left elbow. Palm rests may also be used.

THE SECRET OF STEADY HOLDING

Holding must never be a physical exercise. Do not try to hold by brute strength. Contract your muscles only enough to place your bones in such position that the bones will hold the rifle up. Then relax every other muscle. Particularly have the comb of the stock high enough so that you can lay or rest (not press) your cheek down on it so as to relax the large muscle at the back of the neck and between the shoulder blades (trapezius). Relax all the other muscles also that are not needed to hold the bones in the position. Try to make the bones hold the rifle. Relax, be lazy, be quiet, be slow, be uniform, and thus you will gradually learn to hold steady. He who fusses, frets, screws himself into an uncomfortable position, changes his position, tries to hold by brute strength, never learns to hold steady.

*Rules for competitions and matches will be found in the "Rules for Small Bore Matches," which anyone can obtain for 10 cents by writing to the Secretary, National Rifle Association,

1600 Rhode Island Ave., Washington, D. C. Other rules covering Pistol and Big Bore matches may also be had.

CHAPTER V

TRIGGER SQUEEZE

After you have learned to aim your rifle uniformly, and to hold the rifle steadily in the prone position with the gunsling, the next essential you must master is the trigger squeeze so you can discharge the rifle without disturbing the accurate aim and steady hold. This is one of the most important things in rifle shooting because the natural tendency is to jerk the trigger when the aim is right, and to set the muscles and flinch against the recoil and report which you know is coming, and you will have to train yourself out of these natural tendencies. The difference between the poor and good shots, and between the good and excellent shots, all lies in the relative excellence of their control of the trigger.

Long years of experience in the training of hundreds of thousands of men to shoot the rifle have shown that there is one best way for a beginner to train himself to squeeze the trigger so he will not jerk or flinch. You should squeeze or press it so gradually that you will not know when the rifle is going to fire. Not knowing exactly when the rifle will be discharged, you will not know when to set your muscles against the kick;

that is you will not flinch. Therefore, during the beginning of your practice you should invariably squeeze the trigger in the following manner until it becomes a fixed habit, so you will do it naturally in this way even when you do not think particularly about it.

Assume a correct and steady prone position with the gunsling. You must be able to hold steady in this position before you start to learn trigger squeeze. Aim roughly at the bottom edge of the bull's-eye, forefinger applying a slight pressure on the trigger, enough to take up the slack on the trigger if your trigger has a slack or preliminary pull, but not nearly enough pressure to discharge the rifle. It is best to press or squeeze the trigger with the first joint of the forefinger because this is the most sensitive and delicately trained portion of the human body. Some marksmen prefer to use the second joint. It really does not make much difference which you use. As soon as you become well set in the position, take a deep breath, let the lungs become normal, and then start your effort to hold steadily and aim accurately. When the aim appears to be correct, the front sight having steadied down under and almost touching the bottom of the bull's-eye, very gradually and carefully increase the pressure of your forefinger on the trigger. Increase the pressure ounce by ounce, but *increase it only when the front sight is alined properly on the bottom of the bull's-eye. If, through difficulty in holding, or in seeing the sights, your front sight drifts away from the bottom of the bull, stop increasing the pressure, hold what pressure you have already applied to the trigger by keeping the forefinger immobile, and go on with the increase of pressure, ounce by ounce, only when the front sight is alined correctly again.* During one of the moments when the squeeze or pressure is being increased, and when the sights are correctly alined, the rifle will be discharged more or less unexpectedly. Not knowing exactly when it was going off you did not set your muscles against the kick, did not flinch, and the rifle was not disturbed in its alinement at the critical instant just before the discharge. Then, if the sights were correctly adjusted for range and wind, the bull's-eye will surely be struck.

TRIGGER SQUEEZE EXERCISE

You should practice this trigger squeeze and its co-ordination with holding and aiming in your home for a few days before you begin to shoot on the range with ammunition. To be specific: when you get your first rifle do not rush right out on the range to "try it out". Instead first teach yourself to hold it steadily in the standard prone position with the gunsling. (See Chapter IV.) Then study the sights and aiming. (See Chapter III.) Then start in to practice the trigger squeeze exercise described below for three or four days before you begin to shoot with ammunition. This is the quickest and safest way to learn. Any other way is almost certain to cause you to develop bad habits which must be broken before you can succeed.

Every rifle shot of note practices trigger squeeze exercises. Most really fine shots practice them for fifteen minutes at a time at least two or three times a week. The exercise is done in your home, a small bull's-eye target being tacked on the wall ten feet or more away. The target should be in a good light where it can be seen distinctly, and should be about the same height above the floor that your rifle is when you aim it. Your elbows should be padded, or else a thick mat should be placed on the floor to rest them on to keep them from getting sore. It does no harm to a good rifle to snap it. The following are the details of this exercise when it is done in the prone position:

1. Adjust the gunsling properly, tight enough to give firm support, loop high up on upper arm.

2. Lie down, assume the correct prone position with gunsling, rifle aimed roughly at the target.

3. Place forefinger on trigger with very light pressure, just enough to take up the slack or preliminary pull if the trigger has such a pull, but not nearly enough to discharge the rifle.

4. Take a deep breath, let out about a half of it and then hold the breath.

5. Aim accurately at the bottom edge of the bull's-eye, at the same time holding as steadily as you can.

6. Squeeze or press the trigger slowly, increasing pressure only when the aim is right, holding what pressure you have already applied when the front sight drifts off the bull, and go

ahead with the increase of pressure only when the front sight drifts back to the bull again.

7. Just at or the instant before the rifle "snaps" try to call your shot, that is catch with the eye the exact point where the sights were alined the instant before the trigger gave way, which is the spot where you would expect your bullet to strike the target had the rifle been loaded and the sights correctly adjusted for range and wind.

Take the rifle down from the shoulder and wait a few seconds between each shot. Do not attempt to fire more than 10 shots at a time in these exercises at the start or you will get tired and shaky. Get up, rest a few minutes, then go at it again. Ten to fifteen minutes at a time, twice a day, is as much as you should do of it.

This exercise teaches you not only trigger squeeze, but the proper co-ordination of holding and aiming with the squeeze. We want to impress on you that it is absolutely necessary that you learn this by home practice before you start in to shoot on the range with ammunition, otherwise you will be merely wasting your ammunition and time, and your complete lack of results will discourage you. Likewise it will be very helpful if you practice this exercise regularly even after you have become a good shot.

After two or three weeks of this exercise, combined with range shooting, you will be able to place all but about a couple of ounces of the pressure on the trigger necessary to discharge the rifle as you place your rifle to the shoulder. This greatly quickens the trigger squeeze, and makes it simpler. But you must be careful to squeeze these last ounces on very carefully, and only when the aim is right. After still further practice you seem to be able to often "wish" this last ounce of pressure on the trigger just as the aim is most perfect. Then you have arrived, and see that you continue with these trigger squeeze exercises so that you retain this highly desirable skill.

CHAPTER VI

SIGHT ADJUSTMENT AND RANGE PRACTICE

After you have become fairly proficient in the co-ordination of holding, aiming, and squeezing by practicing the trigger squeeze exercise in your home for a few days, you can then profitably proceed to range practice. At the start this should be conducted similarly to the trigger squeeze exercise. We suggest that you start firing at a range of only 25 yards. At this distance it will be easy for you to surely hit the target, and if you do not have a regular spotting telescope any field glasses or cheap telescope will enable you to see the bullet holes as you shoot, and thus you will not have to leave the firing point and go down to the target to see where you are hitting it until after you have completed firing on all the targets you have placed on the butt. (See Chapter XIII for description of rifle ranges, and instructions for extemporizing ranges.)

Usually rifles are not accurately sighted in at the factory, although an effort is made to have them shoot close to the point of aim at short ranges when the rear sight is set as low as it will adjust, and at zero for windage. Thus it sometimes happens that with normal aim a new rifle will not even hit the entire target at 25 yards when you first start to shoot it. In that case you should lie down at only 10 yards from the target, and fire, say, three shots at it. At this short range these bullets should almost surely strike the target somewhere, no matter how far the sights are from normal adjustment. Now adjust your sights as described below so that when you fire again the bullets will group close to the bottom edge of the bull's-eye. Then go back to the 25-yard firing point and then your shots fired from there with this adjustment of the sights should surely strike somewhere on the 25-yard target. An extemporized target with a black aiming bull's-eye about 2 inches in diameter may be used for this practice, but it will be much more convenient and instructive if you use the standard N. R. A. 75-foot (25-yard) small bore target.

At the start do not endeavor to hit the bull's-eye, but rather try to make a small group of ten shots. Let this group center anywhere on the target. You are really testing out your ability to co-ordinate hold, aim, and squeeze, and do it uniformly. You should keep at this group shooting until you can do these things so well and so uniformly that you can group ten consecutive shots in about a 2-inch circle as shown in Group A on Plate 17. When you can get your group this small it indicates that you are co-ordinating very well for this stage of your practice, and you are ready for your first lesson in sight adjustment which consists of learning how to move your group into the center of the bull's-eye. You should always adjust your sights to do this. Never change your aiming point. (See Chapter III.)

The *point of aim* is the spot on the target where the front sight is alined, usually the bottom edge of the bull's-eye. The *center of impact* is the center of the group on the target where the bullets from an aimed rifle strike. The object of sight adjustment is to make the center of impact come to a certain position with reference to the point of aim. If you aim at the bottom of the bull's-eye, as in Chapter III, you want your center of impact to be a little above the point of aim so that the bullets will strike in the center of the bull's-eye. In hunting it is usually best to have the point of aim and center of impact coincide.

To make your rifle center its shots higher with respect to the point of aim, raise the rear sight. To lower the center of impact, lower the rear sight. (Or move the front sight in the opposite direction.) To make the rifle shoot to the right, move the rear sight to the right, or to move the center of impact to the left, move the rear sight to the left. In other words the general rule is: *"Move your rear sight in the direction in which you wish to move your center of impact"*. Memorize this rule.

Let us now introduce you to a measurement or graduation which is in general use among all modern, well informed rifle shooters. A *minute of angle* or a *minute* as it is called for short, is that graduation or dimension on the rear sight which has an adjusting value of *one inch per hundred yards*. That is, raising your rear sight one minute will raise your center of impact one inch on a target 100 yards away, or 1/4 inch at 25 yards, or 1/2 inch at 50 yards, or 2 inches at 200 yards. Similarly one minute in windage adjustment will move your center of impact horizontally a like amount. Memorize the rule: *"One minute equals one inch per hundred yards"*, and all will be easy.

Now look at Plate 17, the target there illustrated being the standard N. R. A. small bore target. On these targets the scoring rings are always one minute apart. Thus on the 25-yard target the rings are 1/4 inch apart, 50 yards—1/2 inch, and 100 yards—1 inch apart. Notice group A on this plate. The center of the group is 4 rings or minutes below the center of the bull's-eye, and three rings or minutes to the left of the center of the bull. Therefore, if you had been shooting for a small group only, and had just made group A, then if you were to raise your elevation 4 minutes, and move your windage to the right 3 minutes, and then shoot another group of shots, that group would be located something like the group shown in the center of the bull's-eye, and your score would total up to about 97 points.

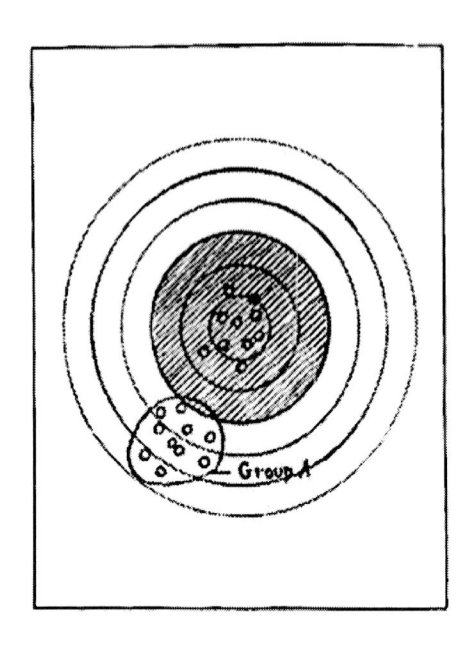

PLATE 17

Let us now look at the sights themselves. Modern sights with minute of angle adjustment operate on the same principle as the machinist's micrometer. Plate 18 shows the elevation scales on such a sight. The lower graduated scale on the slide has lines for each 5 minutes. The graduations around the head of the screw above are for single minutes, with short lines between them for half minutes. There are five graduations of minutes, or ten half minutes, around the circumference of this screw. Turning this screw one complete revolution will raise or lower the elevation five minutes, moving the scale past the pointer on the slide from one graduation to the next five-minute graduation above or below it, depending on which way you turn the screw.

As you turn the screw around you will notice that it "clicks" as it passes each half minute graduation. This is so that you can feel the graduations as well as see them in case you should have to adjust the sight in too dim or glaring light to see the graduations. If you turn the sight four clicks you know you have adjusted it just 2 minutes.

Plate 18 shows the sight adjusted to 5 minutes in elevation, that is 5 minutes on the lower scale, and Zero on the screw. Suppose your sight was set at this elevation when you fired group A shown in Plate 17. Then to raise the sight 4 minutes to bring the center of impact up to a level with the center of the bull, you would turn the screw to the right, clockwise, until the figure 4 on the screw came to the index line, or turn the screw in the same direction 8 clicks. Then the index pointer on the lower scale should be just slightly above the 10-minute line, and the sight would read 9 minutes, that is, considerably over 5 minutes on the slide, and 4 minutes on the screw. If you will take this particular example we have been describing and move the sight on your rifle accordingly, you will get on to the whole thing in a few minutes. The system is exceedingly simple, despite this long description, and once you have become familiar with it all uncertainty as to sight adjustment will disappear. You can move your sight and place your center of impact wherever you want it on the target with absolute certainty.

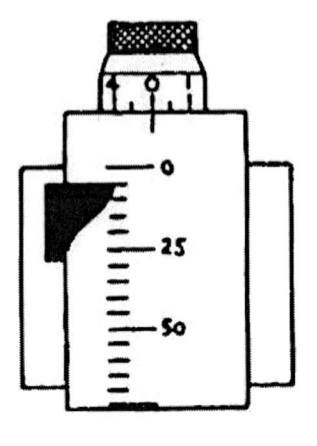

PLATE 18

The windage adjustment works on the same micrometer principle, but the scale is sometimes a little different. Plate 19 shows the usual windage scale. The graduated lines on this scale are 4 minutes apart instead of 5 minutes on the elevation slide. The screw to the left has 8 graduations around its head, each of which clicks. A complete turn of the screw moves the scale one graduation of 4 minutes; therefore, each click on the screw is for a half minute the same as each click on the elevation screw. Plate 19 shows an adjustment of 2 minutes right windage. If your windage was set at this adjustment when you made group A on Plate 17, then you would simply turn the windage screw 6 clicks, moving the sight 3 minutes to the right, to shift the center of impact to a vertical line passing through the center of the bull's-eye.

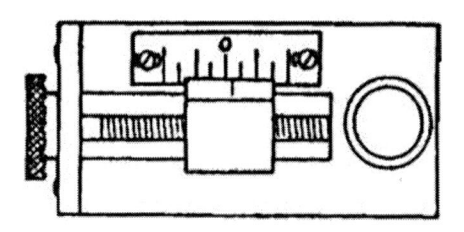

PLATE 19

The reason why these sights are provided with half minute graduations and clicks in addition to those for minutes, is that the accurate rifles and ammunition now provided by our manufacturers will respond to a more accurate adjustment than an inch per hundred yards, and for the finest competitive target shooting we need the refinement of the half minute. Indeed some sights are now being graduated in quarter minutes. The matter of half or quarter minute graduations need not confuse you because they are just a half or a quarter inch per hundred yards.

You will need not only to adjust your sight at the beginning of a score to bring your group into the center of the 10-ring, but also you will frequently have to make minor adjustments during the shooting of a string of ten or twenty shots to keep the shots well into the 10-ring. While a good rifle and ammunition ought to shoot quite consistently to the same spot once it has been warmed up, they do not invariably do so. Also temperature and wind conditions may change while you are firing this string of ten or twenty shots, making a change in sight adjustment desirable.

Thus suppose your first three or four shots strike in the 10-ring, but on looking at the bullet holes through your spotting scope you notice that they are all above the center of the ring. It would now be advisable to reduce your elevation a half minute as you might pull a shot a trifle high, and if so it would probably strike above the 10-ring. This same thing may occur in windage due to a slight increase or decrease in the wind.

As you proceed from shooting at a short range to a longer one you will have to raise the adjustment of the rear sight to compensate for the drop of the bullet. The bullet of the .22 Long Rifle regular velocity cartridge drops from the force of gravity about 8 inches in its flight from 50 to 100 yards, and if you were to fire at 100 yards with the elevation you found correct for 50 yards your bullet would strike the 100-yard target about 8 inches below the center of the bull's-eye. Therefore, you must add about 8 minutes to your 50-yard elevation when shooting at 100 yards, because 8 minutes will raise your center of impact 8 inches at 100 yards.

When you use a rear sight adjusting to minutes you gain

another advantage. The angles of elevation for different ranges have been determined for all cartridges, and having a table of these angles for the cartridge you are using, and having determined your elevation for a given range by shooting at that range, you at once know your approximate elevation for all other distances. For example, here is the table for the .22 Long Rifle cartridges, both regular velocity and the high-speed variety:

ANGLES OF ELEVATION

.22 Long Rifle Cartridges

Range Yards	.22 L. R. Regular M.V. 1100 f.s. Minutes	.22 L. R. Regular M.V. 1100 f.s. Half Minutes or Clicks	.22 L. R. High Speed M.V. 1400 f.s. Minutes	.22 L. R. High Speed M.V. 1400 f.s. Half Minutes or Clicks
25	3.4	6.8	2.3	4.6
50	7.1	14.2	4.7	9.4
75	10.9	21.8	7.5	15.0
100	15.1	30.2	10.5	21.0
125	19.2	38.4	13.7	27.4
150	23.8	47.6	17.2	34.4
175	28.3	56.6	20.7	41.4
200	33.0	66.0	24.6	49.2
225	37.9	75.8	28.4	56.8
250	43.2	86.4	32.6	65.2
275	48.5	97.0	37.0	74.0
300	53.7	107.4	41.3	82.6

To use this table: Suppose you had shot at 50 yards with regular velocity ammunition and found your normal elevation to be 9 minutes. Then for 100 yards your elevation should be about 17 minutes because the table shows that the 100-yard elevation is 8 minutes higher than the 50-yard elevation. Or as the table shows an angle of 7.1 minutes for 50 yards, and the correct angle determined for you and your rifle being 9 minutes, you could simply add 1.9 minutes to all the figures above, and you would have approximately the elevations on your sight for the various distances.

We say "approximately the elevation" because this table will seldom be absolutely correct for every man and rifle. But it will usually be so close that you can set your sights by it and the first shot at the new range will hit in the aiming bull or close to it.

This table has been prepared on the assumption that aim is taken at the center of the bull's-eye. If, however, you aim at 6 o'clock on the bull's-eye of the standard small bore targets, then allowance must be made for the varying radii of the aiming bull's-eyes. Thus in changing from the 3-inch aiming bull at 50 yards to the 6-inch aiming bull's-eye at 100 yards, you must add 1 1/2 minutes or 3 clicks to the difference between the two figures shown in the table to allow for actually aiming 1 1/2 inches further below the center of the bull's-eye on the 100-yard target than you did on the 50-yard target.

While this table is very useful and convenient, the really good shot does not depend much on it. He records all his elevations and windages, together with wind and weather conditions, in his score book. Soon he has records therein for every distance and condition, and from them he can set his sights so accurately that he gets a large percentage of his first shots in the 10-ring. It is impossible to keep all such records in one's head, and the score book is a very necessary help to good shooting.

ADJUSTMENT WITH CRUDE SIGHTS

Unfortunately many shooters buy rifles with crude sights because they are cheaper, not realizing that such sights handicap them so much that really interesting or successful shooting cannot be done with them. Nevertheless, we give you here what rules we can for adjusting such sights, if only to show their shortcomings.

The only rule we can give you for adjusting an open rear sight is the general one: "Move your rear sight the way you want your shot to go". You will have to more or less guess at how much to move it in elevation by means of the little step elevator, and by driving it to the right or left through the barrel slot for windage. Then shoot to see if you have moved it enough, and if not try again. Also the influence of the intensity and direction of light shining on open rear sights is enough to completely upset all calculations, and therefore we have never seen any consistently good shooting, day after day, done with such sights.

If your rear sight is an aperture sight with rather crude sliding scales for elevation and windage, then proceed as follows to determine the rule for its adjustment: Measure the distance between graduations on the scale. This is easiest done by placing a ruler on the scale. If, for example, you find that there are five lines on the scale to every quarter inch on the rule, then the lines are .05 inch apart. Then measure the distance between the front and rear sights. Say you find this to be 28 inches. In 100 yards there are 3,600 inches, which divided by 28 equals 128. Therefore, every move on the rear sight will move the center of impact 128 times that amount on the 100-yard target. The distance between lines on the scale having been found to be .05 inch, multiply this by 128, and we get 6.4 inches. Therefore, for the scale on this sight we have determined the rule: Moving the sight one graduation on the scale moves the center of impact 6.4 inches at 100 yards. Or of course 3.2 inches at 50 yards.

To see these rough scales clearly enough to set the sights with any pretense of accuracy you will usually have to get up from the firing point, hold the sight in a good light close to the eye, and looking carefully at it, count the number of lines from the top of the scale to the index pointer, then loosen the clamping screw, and carefully shove the slide up or down the desired amount, guessing at adjustment between lines. A screwdriver is necessary with some sights to loosen and tighten the windage adjustment. Having moved the sight approximately the desired amount, it will then be necessary to shoot a few shots at the target to see if the adjustment is correct. Of course none of this can be done within the time limit of one minute per shot allowed in target shooting, and such sights are very unsatisfactory for such shooting, or any shooting where any great degree of accuracy is desired.

WIND ALLOWANCE

Wind deflects the bullet from its straight course from muzzle to target, carrying or blowing the bullet with it. Thus a wind from the right will carry a bullet to the left, causing it to strike on the left side of the target. Wind from the rear may very slightly decrease the air resistance, causing a bullet fired over a long distance to strike slightly higher on the target, and a head wind has the opposite effect.

Wind force is measured in miles per hour of its travel. The higher the wind force or velocity the greater the deflection. If the wind velocity is under 3 miles per hour the wind can hardly be felt, and only smoke drift will show it. A wind of 5 miles per hour can be felt on the face, leaves begin to rustle, and it would be called a gentle breeze. At 10 miles per hour leaves and small twigs are in constant motion, light flags are extended, and the wind would be called "fresh". A 15 mile per hour wind begins to raise dust and loose paper, small branches are moved, and the wind would be called "strong". At 20 miles per hour small trees in leaf begin to sway, you jam your hat tighter on your head, and the wind would be called "very strong". At wind velocities over 20 miles per hour it does not pay to shoot with small bore rifles.

Wind direction is indicated by the hours of the clock, assuming that the clock is laid on the range, face up, with 12 o'clock at the target and 6 o'clock at the firing point. Thus a wind blowing directly from the right is a three o'clock wind. Winds from 3 and 9 o'clock give the greatest lateral deviation. Those from 2, 4, 8, and 10 o'clock have about seven-eighths of the deflecting force of 3 and 9 o'clock winds of the same velocity, while those from 1, 5, 7, and 11 o'clock have about one-half the 3 or 9 o'clock deflection.

When you shoot at a certain distance on a very calm day—no appreciable wind—you find that you have to set your wind gauge at a certain reading to strike the center of the bull's-eye. This sight setting then becomes your "zero" windage for that range. It is from this zero that you have to calculate and set your sights for wind allowance. The following table shows the approximate allowance necessary at various distances for winds of certain velocities and directions:

TABLE OF WIND ALLOWANCE

.22 Long Rifle Cartridge, 40-Grain Bullet. M.V. 1100 f.s.

Distance	Miles per Hour	Inches and Minutes Bullet Is Deflected					
		By 1, 5, 7 and 11 o'Clock Winds		By 2, 4, 8 and 10 o'Clock Winds		By 3 and 9 o'Clock Winds	
		Inches	Min.	Inches	Min.	Inches	Min.
50 Yards 1 Minute = ½ Inch	5 10 15 20	.22 .45 .67 .90	.45 .90 1.35 1.80	.38 .78 1.19 1.57	.77 1.57 2.38 3.15	.45 .90 1.35 1.80	.9 1.8 2.7 3.6
100 Yards 1 Minute = 1 Inch	5 10 15 20	.90 1.80 2.70 3.60	.90 1.80 2.70 3.60	1.57 3.15 4.82 6.30	1.57 3.15 4.82 6.30	1.80 3.60 5.40 7.20	1.8 3.6 5.4 7.2
200 Yards 1 Minute = 2 Inches	5 10 15 20	3.60 7.20 10.80 14.40	1.80 3.60 5.40 7.20	6.30 12.60 18.90 25.20	3.15 6.30 9.45 12.60	7.20 14.40 21.60 28.80	3.6 7.2 10.8 14.4

Table is approximately correct for .22 L. R. High-Speed Cartridges also.

Wind correction will always be an estimate as force and direction can never be told exactly and, as a matter of fact, both change slightly every second or so. Set your sights as nearly as you can calculate by the table, hold and squeeze the first shot carefully, note where it struck the target, and then make the necessary sight correction. Afterwards make elaborate notes in your score book, as to the force and direction of the wind, and the amount of wind correction found necessary. With a month or more of such estimating, correcting, and recording you should become a very fair wind doper. Your entries in your score book, if rather elaborately and understandingly kept, will help a lot.

TELESCOPE SIGHTS

Practically every rifle tournament now carries several events in which telescope sights are permitted. Many riflemen whose eyes are no longer sufficiently keen to compete with the younger generation of shooters, using iron sights, find that with a good telescope sight their ability to score well has diminished little if any. Telescope sights at their best are slightly more accurate than iron sights as they practically eliminate the errors of aim. A good telescope sight score will usually have more shots in the X-ring than will an iron sight score.

Several splendid American made telescope sights are available, such as the Fecker, Lyman, and Unertl. They are made with various powers of magnification from 3 to 16. The 10 power glass is the one most generally used for small bore target shooting. Glasses can be had with objective lenses from 3/4 inch to 1 1/2 inches. Those with the smaller diameters are entirely satisfactory, but the larger the objective the brighter is the view through the scope, and the more effectively it can be used for spotting shots in the target. The reticule should be the "medium" or "medium fine" cross hair.

All the above telescopes are equipped with double

micrometer mounts adjustable for both elevation and windage. Screwing out (counter clockwise—up) on the top micrometer screw results in taking higher elevation. Screwing out (counter clockwise—right) on the right hand micrometer screw results in taking windage to the right, and vice versa. The stems of the screws are graduated with lines 25 half minutes apart, and the barrels of the screws are graduated with lines half minutes apart. In addition the best mounts have quarter minute clicks, the barrel clicking for each half minute and also between each half minute. To read a telescope sight mount, if, for example, two graduations are in sight on the stem (50 half minutes), and the barrel reads halfway between 15 and 16, the reading is 65 1/2 half minutes. The value of these adjustments is as stated only when the distance between the centers of the base blocks on the barrel of the rifle is 7.2 inches. Bases are so located on most of the best small bore target rifles.

In order that the mountings can be set at the location of these bases, and also that the eyepiece can be adjusted about 2 inches in front of one's eye when one assumes the standard firing positions, it is necessary that the tube of the telescope sight be at least about 18 inches long. A collar encircles the tube just in front of the front mount, and can be clamped in position with a screw. Each time the rifle is fired the scope tube recoils slightly forward, and it should be pulled back before the next shot until this collar abuts against the front of the front mount to insure that the scope will be the proper and uniform distance from the eye.

Proper focusing of the telescope sight is essential for accurate results and to avoid eyestrain, and the instructions furnished by the manufacturers should be carefully read and followed.

The above makes of telescope sights can be readily removed from the rifle by merely unscrewing the clamping screws and sliding the mounts off their bases, when the iron sights can be used. The telescopes can then be replaced again in about a minute in perfect adjustment.

Usually a higher comb is desirable on the stock when telescope sights are used. This can be easily accomplished by lacing a Jotsam or Stam Monte Carlo cheek pad on the stock when the scope is used, and removing it when iron sights are used.

CHAPTER VII

SLOW FIRING

In slow fire target shooting we have ample opportunity to train ourselves in all those things that are necessary for accurate shooting. We know the exact distance to the target, we have a well-defined black bull's-eye on a white background to aim at, we see where each bullet strikes the target, and we have plenty of time to correct our errors* and to perfect ourselves in the execution of each detail. This is what slow fire is for—the perfection of each detail, so that practical shooting, which we will take up later, will be more accurate and effective. Thus our constant endeavor in slow fire is to do everything so perfectly and so uniformly that a high score will result—to place every bullet in the 10-ring in the center of the aiming bull's-eye.

In the United States, slow fire shooting with .22 caliber rifles is conducted in accordance with rules prescribed by the National Rifle Association. The distances are usually 50 and 75 feet indoors, and 50, 100, 150, 175, 200, and 300 yards on outdoor ranges. The targets used are the standard National Rifle Association small bore targets, there being a different target for each distance. (See Chapter XII for description of targets.) Such shooting is usually conducted by rifle clubs that are affiliated with the National Rifle Association on their home ranges. Competitions are held among their own members or with other clubs. There are also regional and state competitions, and the National Rifle Association holds indoor and outdoor mail matches and stages large national competitions at various ranges such as Camp Ritchie and Camp Perry. It is a great advantage to the shooter to join a club affiliated with the National Rifle Association and shoot with them, because he is then able to use their well-equipped range, and he learns a lot by association with the good shots in the club. But if a shooter is so situated that he cannot join a club it is not difficult to quickly build a small bore range almost anywhere in farming country, and to practice alone on such a range. This handbook and the advanced works on marksmanship are an aid to one who has to train himself without the aid of a coach. While such a lone shooter cannot compete shoulder to shoulder with others, he can compete with world's record scores, and it is entirely possible for him to develop his shooting ability in this manner, alone on his own range, so that he can visit the big national competitions with as good a chance of winning as anyone.

Thus if you want to excel with the rifle get a range, even if you have to build it yourself, study this handbook and indulge in home practice until you know the theoretical side, and then get all the practical shooting you can on the range, preferably one morning or afternoon a week if you can afford that much time. About two months of careful weekly practice should make you into a very fair shot, but to reach and stay in the expert class requires much longer. Indeed progress is very analogous to that in learning to play golf, no harder, and no easier, but containing a little simple mechanics and science which make a particular appeal to the majority of our boys and men.

We shall assume that you have a suitable rifle range available. Before you leave your home for the range, wipe all the oil out of the bore and chamber of your rifle, because the first few shots from a clean, oily bore are liable to fly a little wild. Also check over and see that you have the following material with you—nothing forgotten:

Rifle with bolt in it and sights on it. Score book and pencil.
Ammunition. Forked rifle rest.
Spotting scope and stand. Cartridge block.

Shooting coat and glove.

The following material may also be necessary, depending on conditions:

Paper targets, tacks, and small hammer.
Canvas sheet to lie on (damp or dirty ground).
Telescope sight.
Shooting spectacles.
Tool kit.

Advanced shooters usually carry all these articles, except rifle and shooting coat, in a small satchel or metal box termed a "Dope Bag".

On arriving at the range the first thing to do is to look at the wind and weather conditions and set your sights. If you have not previously fired at this distance then you should proceed as indicated in Chapter VI. But if you have done considerable shooting with your rifle and ammunition then you should turn to your score book, see if you can find in it a sheet where you fired at this same distance under the same weather and wind conditions as now pertain, and set your sights at the elevation and windage that proved correct on that occasion. Then record the sight setting, together with the distance you are shooting at, wind and weather conditions, and details of rifle and ammunition on a blank page in your score book. (See Plate 21.) Then smoke your sights black so they will not glisten. This may be done in the flame of burning camphor, a small acetylene lantern, a candle, or even a match, wiping oil off the sights before attempting to blacken them. Do not blacken ivory or red bead sights.

SLOW FIRE PRONE

When the range officer tells you that a certain target is available for you to fire on, go to that firing point, set up your spotting scope trained and focused on your target, and place your forked rifle rest, cartridge block with the required number of cartridges in it, score book and pencil in position. Adjust the gunsling on your arm, then lie down ready to fire. In this position everything should be arranged in a convenient and methodical manner. (See Plate 20.) The spotting scope is set up so that it is just to the right or left of the barrel of your aimed rifle, but not so close as to interfere with free holding. The forked rifle rest is in the ground a little to the right of where your left hand is when aiming, and the score book and cartridge block are convenient to your right hand. Thus, when you fire a shot you can lower your rifle into the rifle rest, and leaning your head a little to one side, bring your eye into the field of view of the spotting scope without disturbing your position on the ground.

PLATE 20—Everything in Its Proper Place

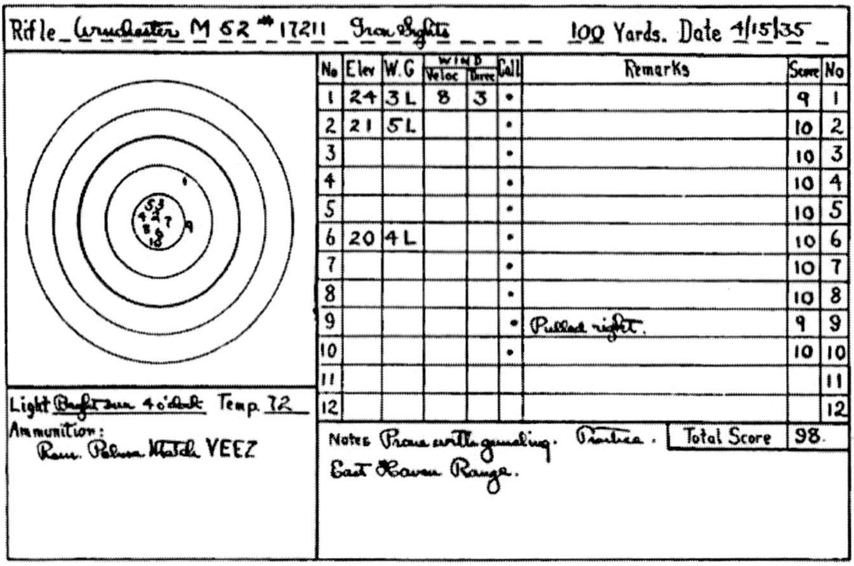

PLATE 21—Score Sheet, Slow Fire Prone

Get everything arranged systematically and your position correct before you start to fire. This is very important. Place your rifle to your shoulder, sling correct, aim at the target, and see if your position is correct and comfortable. If not, shift the position a little until it is right. Note where your elbows rest on the ground and make little holes there for them so they will not slip out of position. Then do not get out of this position or vary it a particle while you are firing your string of ten or twenty rounds. It is necessary, of course, to bring your rifle down into the rest after each shot, and to lean over to see through the spotting scope, but any other movements should be avoided, so that each time you put the butt of the rifle to your shoulder to aim it comes to as identically the same position as you can make it—same lie on the ground, same tension on gunsling, elbows at same spot on the ground. Uniform and accurate shooting requires uniform holding. The shooter who fidgets around on the firing point, or who gets up and lies down again after he has started his string, gets a miserable score, and at once publishes the fact that he is a tyro.

Everything about your position being correct, place the rifle to your shoulder, looking for and aiming at your own targets,* steady down, perfect your aim and squeeze off as carefully and correctly as you can. Call your shot. Then methodically lower your rifle into the forked rifle rest which takes its weight off your arms and prevents fatigue, lean over to the spotting scope, look at your target, note where the bullet has struck, then place a figure 1 on the target diagram on your score sheet to indicate where the first shot struck. (See Plate 21.)

If this first shot did not strike where you called it, then you should make the necessary correction in sight adjustment. Assume now that you are firing the score shown on Plate 21 at 100 yards. It is a sunny spring day with an 8-mile wind from 3 o'clock,˙ and for your first shot you have set your elevation at 24 half minutes or clicks, and your wind gauge at 3 half minutes or clicks left. You call your first shot a bull, and you therefore place a small dot in the center of the square in the "Call" column. When you look through your spotting scope you see that the bullet has struck in the 9 ring at 1 o'clock* and you place a figure 1 on the target diagram. Now you change your sight adjustment to elevation 21 and windage 5 left, because this lowering of 3 half minutes or clicks will lower your next shot 1 1/2 inches, or 1 1/2 rings, which is just how much too high your first shot struck; and moving the wind gauge 2 half minutes left will bring your next shot just 1 inch or 1 ring to the left, which is just how much your first shot struck to the right of the center of the bull's-eye. Your second, third, fourth, and fifth shots are now fired under identical conditions, and all strike in the 10 ring, but you will note that your group is forming in the upper left-hand section of the 10 ring. It is not safe to let it form so far from the center, because there is danger of a shot going out. So you lower your elevation a half minute or half inch to 20, and also move your wind gauge a half minute right. Your sixth, seventh, and eighth shots, all of which are called bulls, center well in toward the center of the 10 ring. On the ninth shot you get a bad pull when the front sight appeared a little to the right of directly under the bull, and, sure enough, when you look through your spotting scope you see your bullet hole in the 9 ring over at 3 o'clock. Of course, this is just where you pulled it, and no change in sight setting is indicated, so you are more careful how you pull your last shot, get it off perfectly, and it lands well into the 10 ring. Afterwards, when you have time, you add up your score which totals 98, a fine average score for a very good shot.

It is a very great advantage to record every score you fire in this perfect manner. You can get to know your rifle thoroughly in no other way. There are too many of these data for any man to remember. The shooter who trusts to memory is continually making mistakes which lower his scores and his season's average, and particularly he does not know his rifle well enough to often get a "10" for the first shot. If you keep your score book conscientiously you will win out in the end. This score sheet now gives you a most perfect guide for the next time that you come to shoot this rifle and ammunition at 100 yards.

SLOW FIRE, SITTING

Here the procedure is almost exactly the same as when shooting prone. The spotting scope is set up to the right so you can lean over and look through it when necessary. The forked rifle rest is seldom used as it is easy to rest the rifle in the lap between shots. Select your ground so that if possible you sit on a spot a little higher than the spots where your heels rest, as this gives you a steadier position. You cannot hold sitting quite as steadily as you can prone, and a lot of nice concentration and co-ordination is necessary to get the trigger squeezed off during one of the periods when the front sight has drifted or is lingering just right under the bull. Call every shot, and note the calls in the proper column on your score sheet.

We usually shoot sitting only at the shorter distances, and it is not customary to spot each shot on the score sheet. You usually start out knowing your sight adjustment pretty well from having previously fired at this distance in the prone position. Every two or three shots, however, you should lean over and look through the spotting scope. If your shots are not going where you call them you should make the necessary correction in sight adjustment. Then when you finish your score, get up and go back of the firing point, sit down, and complete all necessary entries in the score book. Particularly put down just what sight adjustment proved best, and the wind and weather conditions, rifle and ammunition used, and the fact that the score was shot sitting. Sometimes in shooting sitting a shooter will find that he requires one or two half minutes sight adjustment higher than is correct when he fires prone at the same distance. This is because, not being quite so steady, he does not aim with the top of his front sight quite so close to the bottom of the bull, and he has to take a little more elevation to compensate for it—that is he aims lower, and has to increase his elevation slightly to make the bullet hit high enough.

SLOW FIRE, KNEELING

In general the same instructions pertain as for shooting

sitting. There is usually a tendency to swing from side to side when aiming, and one must try to overcome this, and also to time his squeeze carefully to get off when the front sight is drifting under the bull. Much practice kneeling is necessary to limber up the right knee so one does not get cramped in the position. At first it may be necessary to stand up once or twice during the string to relieve the pain in the knee. Some shooters with limber knee joints do not have this trouble at all.

SLOW FIRE, STANDING

This is the most difficult of all manners of firing the rifle, and the one taking the longest practice in which to become proficient; and yet it is always the position first attempted by the beginner who has no coach or manual to start him off right. His total lack of results too often discourages him so that he soon quits the game. And yet no other form of shooting gives quite so much satisfaction to the shooter once he has learned to excel in it.

It is best not to start shooting standing on the range until you have done several weeks of conscientious trigger squeeze exercises in this position at home, because at the start your inability to hold the rifle with anything that approaches steadiness will be very discouraging. When you first start these standing exercises in all probability your front sight will wander all around the target like the thin line in Cut A, Plate

22. But two weeks of these exercises will narrow your tremors to something like that shown in Cut B, and then you can profitably start with your range shooting.

You should start this shooting in a slow, almost phlegmatic manner. Do not exert yourself, or hurry, or get in the least excited. Some of the best shots we know have a camp stool at the firing point and sit down between shots. It is a great advantage to call and spot each shot. For this purpose either have your spotting scope on a high tripod, or else have a friend at the scope, call your shot to him, and let him note your call and the location of your hit in your score book. When you get to the point where your bullets are striking close to where you call them you are making real progress, and incidentally you know that your sight adjustment is absolutely correct.

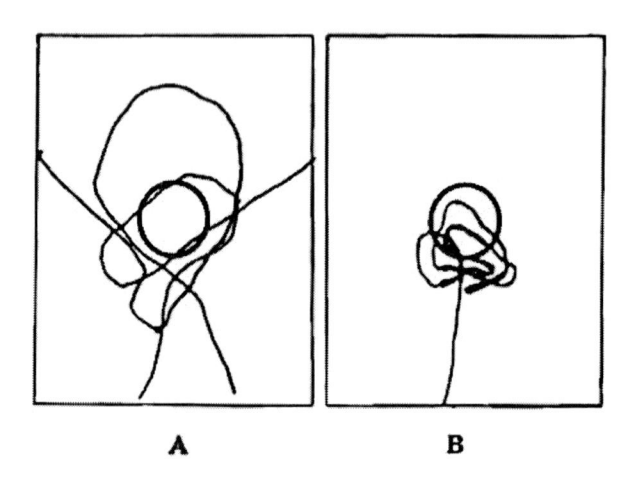

A   B

PLATE 22—Tremors of Front Sight

Now look again at Cut B, Plate 22. You are making an effort to get the final squeeze on the trigger when your front sight is in those parts of its tremors represented by the heavier portions of the line, that is, while the front sight is hugging around the bottom of the bull. At first you cannot do this, but don't get discouraged, keep on trying. Gradually your rifle will swing or tremble more slowly. Before long you will have co-ordinated so that you are putting your increase of squeeze on the trigger as the front sight swings under the bull. Soon you can do it two or three times in ten shots, and then a greater number, and the first thing you know you are getting good scores, and you have arrived.

As you attempt to hold and squeeze you will find that it often takes a long time to get the shot off. In such cases your hold may become shaky before you manage to get the final squeeze. If so don't fire, but bring the rifle down, sit down and wait a minute or so before starting again. Gradually, however, try to get your shot off within 10 to 15 seconds of the moment when you begin to aim. The slow, poky shooter seldom becomes a really good offhand shot. Keep cool, don't hurry, but don't poke too much either. If you shoot on the range once a week, then at least two other periods of twenty minutes of trigger squeeze exercises at home will help your progress a lot. Don't expect to get scores up in the eighties your first season's practice—very few can do that.

All of the above description is for shooting in the "Army

Standing" position as described in Chapter IV, with the left upper arm and elbow free from the body. There is another standing position known as the "N. R. A. Standing" position (see Plate 16), in which the left elbow is rested on the advanced hip, and the rifle is either balanced on the finger tips, or held by a palm rest. This position is permitted in "Free Rifle Shooting" and in many N. R. A. competitions. It is steadier than the standard offhand position, but it is not suited for practical shooting—rapid fire and snap shooting.

WHAT TO EXPECT

If you are a beginner you will naturally want to know how well you are progressing at various stages of your practice. If you scan the scores made in the big matches you will note that the winners usually get possible scores of 100 at all ranges when shooting prone, about 96 to 97 when sitting, and about 80 to 85 standing. Don't expect to average anywhere near this the first season. The shooters who win matches with such scores have been playing the game for all they are worth for several years at least. Moreover, they don't win or make scores like these every time. The winners in a match are the topnotchers who are particularly lucky on that day, and their high scores do not represent their regular average, which is slightly lower.

Shooting prone, if you have carefully studied all the fine points we have been trying to tell you about and done your best to apply them, in about a month you should be averaging scores around 90 to 95. A month more and you are running around 93 to 96 in good weather. Towards the end of your first season you ought to be making around 95 to 99. Perhaps a few of you will average 97 to 99, and get an occasional possible. If so, you are getting close to competition form for prone shooting.

In the sitting position scores around 85 are excellent for the first two or three months, and anything over 92 is splendid towards the end of the first season. Kneeling scores ought to run about five points lower.

Your progress will probably be much slower standing. At the start you will do well to keep all ten shots on the target. After two months you should be running scores somewhere around seventy-five. Perhaps if you are specially gifted you may get up almost to an average of 80 towards the end of your first season. A shooter who averages much over 80 points standing has not only been doing a lot of conscientious work, but he is more or less gifted in his ability to co-ordinate. We do not see many such men.

* It is very easy, if you do not watch it constantly, to fire on some other shooter's target, which seores you a penalty point, and often gets you a good cussing out.

* Direction on both the target and range is designated as with a clock, the top of the target being 12 o'clock, and the right side of the target being 3 o'clock. On the range the target is at 12 o'clock and the firing point at 6 o'clock, and a wind blowing straight across the range from the right is a 3 o'clock wind.

* In practice shooting in slow fire there is no time limit. In record shooting or in competitions the time limit is 45 seconds per shot, or an aggregate of 7 1/2 minutes for ten shots, counting from the time the target is ready to fire on until the last shot, at all ranges up to and including 100 yards, and 1 minute per shot at longer ranges.

CHAPTER VIII

RAPID FIRE

Although we have made a sport of it, theoretically at least, slow fire is instructional fire in which the shooter learns to fire accurately and consistently, and to hit the object he aims at at known distances. All practical firing in sport is more or less rapid fire. Therefore, as soon as you have become skilled in slow fire, you should take up rapid fire and make yourself proficient in it as well. Rapid fire is not different from slow fire except in that it is performed more rapidly, usually it being required that the five shots contained in the magazine be fired within 30 seconds or less, instead of the time limit of one minute per shot in slow fire. Thus rapid fire involves a faster, but if possible no less accurate, performance of assuming the firing position, aiming, squeezing, and then a rapid but sure manipulation of the breech action of the rifle for the next shot.

It is very desirable that you practice the following rapid fire exercise in your home with empty rifle until you have acquired the skill to perform it quickly, surely, without fumbling, and in a more or less subconscious manner. While it is possible to considerably quicken the operation of loading a single shot rifle, yet in general, rapid fire can be executed only with a repeating or magazine rifle. Most bolt action magazine rifles have magazines which contain five cartridges. Therefore, in small bore shooting rapid fire consists of firing two strings of five shots each within a time limit of thirty seconds per string. Sufficient time is given between the two strings to permit you to refill your magazine. Being at the firing point, magazine filled, one cartridge loaded into the chamber, safety lock turned to "Safe" and rifle in the position of "Ready" (butt below the shoulder), the range officer gives the command "Commence Firing", and thirty or twenty seconds later the command "Cease Firing". At the command "Commence Firing" you turn your safety to "Ready", assume the firing position, aim at your target, and endeavor to fire five shots within the time limit. For every shot fired by you before or after the commands, ten points will be deducted from your score. The regular slow fire target is usually used. Rapid fire may be held in the standing, kneeling, sitting, or prone positions as prescribed. This in general is the procedure, although it may differ a little on various ranges and in certain matches.

    Rapid fire should always start with the safety of the rifle turned to "Safe" because skill and speed in unlocking the rifle is an essential part of rapid fire. The rifle should always be operated without removing it from the shoulder, or from the firing position. Relinquish the grip of the right hand on the stock, grasp the knob of the bolt handle with the thumb and two fingers, lift and pull back the bolt smartly, quickly, but surely, doing this seemingly all in one motion rather than first a lift up and then a pull back. Then at once shove the bolt forward and turn it down, also all in one motion. Make these movements complete, quick, and smooth, with enough force to insure their positiveness. Then regrasp the stock, finger on the trigger, and enough pressure on the trigger to surely take up any slack in the trigger. The rifle will now be swaying from side to side as a result of this operation. Stop this swinging at once so you can aim by pressing the cheek against the left side of the comb of the stock, and the ball of the thumb against the right, lower, front side of the comb. This pressure from two sides is merely a part of assuming the firing position again, no alteration of the position being made to exercise this squeeze which stops the swinging.

In operating the mechanism in the prone and sitting positions, turn or cant the rifle a little to the right as you open your bolt, and straighten the rifle up as you close the bolt. Also carry the left hand slightly down and to the right as you open the bolt, and bring it up and to the left into aiming position as you close the bolt. Keep both elbows in their holes in the ground, or on your knees, and the sling in proper position on the arm all the time.

In the kneeling and standing positions, as the right hand

lets go of the stock to operate the bolt, pull back hard on the rifle with the left hand to keep the butt of the rifle in position on the shoulder. Operate the bolt without canting the rifle, or lowering the left hand, keeping the rifle fairly well aimed toward the target while operating. Of course you must always carry your head a trifle to the left when opening the bolt to prevent your cheek being struck by the bolt as it is withdrawn.

Always keep your eye on your target (your own target too) while operating the rifle. Never look at the rifle to see the bolt operate and the cartridge go in. This is most important. If you do not keep your eye on the target your rapid fire will be very slow, and you will lose your target, or fire on the wrong target continually.

Now practice this operation of the bolt for a few minutes, doing it exactly as above, slowly at first, reading the instructions over a number of times to be sure you get it exactly as described in every detail. When you have learned the movement, begin to practice the rapid fire exercise as described below, learning it first in the prone position, then sitting, kneeling, and finally standing. Continue practicing the exercise until you have become proficient, sure, and quick before finally taking up rapid fire on the range with ammunition.

RAPID FIRE EXERCISE

Start with rifle locked, sling on the arm (except standing

position), rifle in ready position, butt below the shoulder, eyes on the target.

1. Assume the firing position, unlocking rifle at the same time, place enough pressure on the trigger to take up any slack, aim at the target, steady down, then squeeze the trigger as soon as aim appears correct. Hasten these operations but without sacrificing accurate aim and careful squeeze. It is usually best to swing the front sight from one side to its alinement under the bull, and to try to time the squeeze so the rifle goes off as the front sight gets squarely below the bull. Usually this will result in a larger proportion of hits than were you to try to raise the front sight from below and fire as it almost touches the bull.

2. At once let go with the right hand and operate the bolt quickly and surely as described above. Regrasp the small of the stock and stop the swing of the rifle by pressure between cheek and ball of the thumb. Take up any slack on the trigger, start aim, and continue as in Paragraph 1 until five shots have been fired. Then rest a couple of minutes before repeating.

Do not time yourself at first. Do not attempt to do the operations so quickly that you fumble. Make every operation correctly, and gain speed slowly. Never hasten the aim and trigger squeeze, but get these as perfect as possible every time. When you think you are beginning to get fair rapidity, with perfection in all details, have someone time you, giving the commands for commencing and ceasing firing, and also call out each five seconds so you will know how the time is going. If you are practicing alone have a clock with a large second hand immediately above your aiming target. Stick to 30 seconds for a long time before attempting the 20 second time limit. And do not attempt rapid fire on the range with ammunition until you are satisfied that you have developed a sure, quick performance of all the essentials. All of this is much simpler than it sounds. Very fair rapidity and surety can be acquired in about five practice periods of about 15 minutes each.

The one big stumbling block in rapid fire is the tendency to snatch or jerk at the trigger just as soon as the sights appear aimed with anything near to correctness. You must constantly fight against this tendency at first. Strive for a correct trigger squeeze, try to put all the pressure on the trigger you dare, and then carefully squeeze on the last ounce as the front sight drifts below the bull's-eye. This is not very difficult either. You soon learn it, but learn it you must if you would do well at rapid fire.

CHAPTER IX

TOURNAMENTS AND COMPETITIONS

After you have become proficient in slow fire and have mastered the instructions given up to this point, you will, no doubt, be taking part in the shoots at your local club and enjoying the pleasures of shoulder to shoulder competition. Use the first opportunity to go to some larger competition or tournament, and though you may not win a prize the first time, you need to take part in such tournaments to overcome the "buck fever" which afflicts all beginners at such shoots.

At these larger tournaments you will have a chance to meet the topnotchers of the shooting game and to observe the way they do things. You will see all sorts of strange gadgets for which great claims are made, but above all you will have a chance to mingle with and make the acquaintance of the best bunch of sportsmen anywhere.

You may hesitate to go to such a tournament for fear of doing the wrong thing or of making yourself conspicuous because of your ignorance of the customs and manners of such affairs. Do not let this deter you, but read on and we will try to point out some of the things you should do and besides you will find the staff and the competitors most considerate to the beginner and very willing to explain and assist.

The National Rifle Association through its system of Registered Tournaments and nation-wide classification of shooters makes it possible for you to find a small bore tournament within easy driving distance of your home almost any week-end. "Registered Tournaments" are all conducted under identical rules and each one is umpired by an N. R. A. Official Referee. All scores are immediately reported to the Association and shooters from Maine to Hawaii are classified under a uniform system based on their scores in actual competition. The N. R. A. will be glad to furnish you with complete information on how the classification system works. By reference to "The American Rifleman" each month you can learn where and when Registered Tournaments are going to be held during the two months ahead.

Small bore rifle shooting, through the organization provided by the National Rifle Association, boasts as complete a list of championship events as any sport in America. At the top are the International Rifle Teams, next the annual National Championships, then Regional Championships, below them come District and State Championships, and finally the local registered tournaments for city and county titles.

Suppose you decide to attend the five day tournament of the Eastern Rifle and Pistol Association at Camp Ritchie, Maryland, over the Fourth of July. You find that the shoot is to run July 1st to 5th, inclusive, and that you will be able to go on July 2nd. Of course, you will want to shoot the first day you arrive, so read the program carefully and either mail your entry for your first day's matches or be prepared to pay post entry fees for that day.

When you arrive in camp you should first register, giving full information as to name, address, rifle club, the type and make of the gun and ammunition you will use. You will then be assigned a competitor number by which you will be known at this tournament. You will also be assigned tent or quarters if available and told where you may draw bedding, etc. You will be charged a registration fee, usually one dollar. After you have located your place in camp and gotten your bedding arranged, it is well to go next to the Entry Office and make entries in all the single entry matches you wish to enter. At the large tournaments there are two types of competition; single entry matches, in which you shoot a prescribed course once and re-entry matches in which you may shoot the same course a number of times and in which the aggregates of your best two or three or five targets count. Matches may be either squadded or unsquadded. If squadded this means that you will be expected to fire your score on a designated target at some specified time. This target and time is given to you on what is called a squadding ticket. These are usually distributed by the Entry Office on the evening before a match is fired or at least two hours before the scheduled time of starting the match. Unsquadded matches are those which may be fired at any time that targets are available during the tournament.

When you have made your entries in the various single entry matches you will get a receipt showing the matches entered. Save it for your own information and as a check to prove your entry, should it get misplaced.

Before leaving the Statistical Office buy a re-entry or practice ticket as available for each range and keep it in your shooting kit. You never can tell when it may be necessary to check your sighting at some range because of some accident to equipment, and when such emergencies arise, there is seldom time to go back and get re-entry tickets for this purpose.

When the time arrives for your first match, look at the Squadding Ticket which you have previously obtained at the Entry Office and you will generally find on it a target number, a relay number and a time. Let us say it reads, "Target 27, relay 2, time $\frac{8.40}{2}$." This means that one relay of shooters will fire before you do. Go to a point back of firing point 27 about $\frac{8.15}{2}$ after checking that you have all of your equipment and when you have located your place on the line as shown by a numbered stake on the firing point, there are two or three things to do. See that your sights are set properly for elevation and windage and that your spotting scope is mounted on the tripod and adjusted. Also note that you have the bolt in your rifle—it is amazing how many get lost or misplaced at a tournament. Count out the number of cartridges you will need for this stage of the match and put them in your loading block and when the order is given for the second relay to get on the line move up and take your place on the firing line. These preliminary preparations will give you more time to select a satisfactory position and get set to go before you hear the command "Commence Firing". After the targets have been changed and your targets put up, the Range Officer will give the command "Commence Firing". It is common practice to allow some interval of time before record fire starts in which you will be permitted to fire fouling shots and in most matches five sighting shots. Fouling shots are not aimed but are fired rapidly into the ground in front of the firing point or into the backstop and serve to warm up the gun and to deposit a uniform fouling in the barrel. It has been found that unless five or more fouling shots are so fired through a barrel it will tend to show a gradual change of elevation on the first few shots for record and thus spoil what would otherwise be a good score.

In small bore matches it is customary to permit five sighting shots, on a target placed above the record targets, to check sight setting and to facilitate adjustments for effect of wind and light conditions.

Be careful to avoid hitting the record targets with either the fouling or sighting shots—if this happens have the range officer inspect and note it before you start your record string. When you have fired the required number of shots—you should use a loading block to insure this and be sure to fire at your own target—do not get up and leave the line until the shooters on either side of you have completed their scores as you may disturb them; when they are done or on command move off the firing line quietly after cleaning up for the next man.

If firing at long ranges where targets are operated from a pit, each shot will be marked from the pit and signalled to the scorer who announces the number of the shot and its value and posts it on a score board. It is your job to see that he announces and posts the value correctly. If he makes a mistake, call the Range Officer and get it corrected before firing again. No correction will be made after you fire the next shot.

THE BULLETIN BOARD

At every tournament shoot you will find a Bulletin Board on which are posted scores and other official notices. It is the duty of the competitor to consult the Bulletin Board at least twice a day, since changes in the program and rules will be posted here and the management have given full notice of changes, etc., if they are posted on the board. After you completed your scores in the match the targets are taken in and scored and the Statistical Office will post them as quickly as feasible. There are three kinds of bulletins, Reveille, Preliminary and Official bulletins. The Reveille Bulletin will usually show no names except the name and number of the match and will be posted by relays in target order. You will look at the sheet for Relay 2, target 27, and see that the score posted agrees with the score you recorded in your Score Book. If it does not agree and you had no doubtful shots, you should question it by indicating the mistake to the Statistical Office.

Shortly after all targets are scored the Statistical Office will post a Preliminary Bulletin showing the scores ranked according to the rules. If the score you make would entitle you a listing on the Preliminary Bulletin and your name does not appear, you should file a protest in the manner provided for in the program and in Official Rules.

The Preliminary Bulletin will carry a notation of the hour of posting and fix some time from 4 to 12 hours later, after which no protests will be received. If there is a mistake, make your protest known at once or you may forfeit your right to make one.

After the period noted on the Preliminary Bulletin has expired, an Official Bulletin will be posted showing winners, their scores and prizes, medals, etc. Medals and trophies are generally distributed at a meeting at the end of the shoot, though custom varies on this and they may be available as soon as the Official Bulletins are posted.

When the time comes to go home, clean up your quarters and turn in any equipment you have drawn and go on home. You will have made a flock of new acquaintances and friends, and when the next opportunity arises you will be back again to enjoy the thrill of competition with the best of the shooters in the territory, the chance to improve your ability and knowledge of the game on the firing line and in the bullfests in the evening and by association with a group of true sportsmen.

CHAPTER X

FIELD SHOOTING

All of the shooting we have considered so far has been what is known as "known distance shooting", that is the distance to the target is known exactly, and the sights can be set in advance for that distance so that with correct aim the bull's-eye will be struck somewhere near its center. In practical field shooting, however, the distance to the target is seldom known exactly, but must be estimated, and either the sights must be set quickly for that estimated distance, or else they must be set in advance for some certain distance over which the trajectory is known intimately, and allowance must then be made for the rise or fall of the bullet above or below the line of aim at the estimated distance. Here we depart from our previous rule that aim is always taken with the front sight almost touching the bottom of the bull's-eye, and we often aim a little high or low to allow for the trajectory.

At this stage, therefore, it is desirable for you to know the trajectory of the .22 Long Rifle cartridge, both the regular and the high-speed varieties. These trajectories are the same in all rifles—the cartridge, not the rifle, determining the trajectory.

The trajectory or path of the bullet through the air is always curved like that of any object thrown through the air. The amount of the curve over a certain distance is designated by the number of inches the bullet rises above a straight line joining the muzzle of the rifle and the bullet hole in the target, this distance being usually called the "mid-range height of trajectory". For example, in shooting at 100 yards with the cartridge of regular velocity the bullet rises to a height of 4.2 inches above an imaginary line connecting muzzle and target, and for the high-speed cartridge this height is 3 inches, as shown on Plate 23.

The sights, however, stand above the barrel, and the line of aim is considerably above the axis of the bore from which this trajectory given in the usual tables is figured. This makes considerable difference in the practical trajectory above the line of aim, which is the trajectory we want to know for practical purposes. Let us say that the height of the front sight above the axis of the bore on your rifle is 3/4 inch. In Plate 23 the heavy cross-section lines indicate 5 yards horizontally and 1 inch vertically. "M" is the muzzle of the rifle and "T" is the target. The line M-T is the base line from muzzle to target above which the trajectory curve is determined and plotted as shown.

Now take a point 3/4 inch above M, and that is where your line of aim starts if your front sight is 3/4 inch above the axis of the bore. Suppose you sight in your rifle to strike the exact point of aim at 60 yards. Then a line drawn from the 3/4-inch high point, which we will call "S", through the 60-yard point on the trajectory curve will be your line of aim for figuring your practical trajectory, and from this line you can then measure how far above or below the line of aim your bullets will strike at all distances, merely measuring vertically from the line of aim to the trajectory curve on the chart.

For example, with the regular velocity cartridge we see from Plate 23 that if we set our sights for 60 yards so as to strike the point of aim at that distance (strike the bull's-eye at 6 o'clock when aiming at 6 o'clock), then at 35 yards our bullet will strike 1 inch above the line of aim, at 71 yards it will strike 1 inch below the line of aim, at 80 yards 2 inches low, at 90 yards 4 inches low, and at 100 yards it drops about 6 1/2 inches low. Thus if your sights were set for 60 yards, and you suddenly had to fire on a target that you estimated to be 90 yards away, you would need to aim 4 inches above it to strike it. Also with your sights set for 60 yards you can aim directly at an object, and you will not miss it by more than an inch all the way from the muzzle to 71 yards.

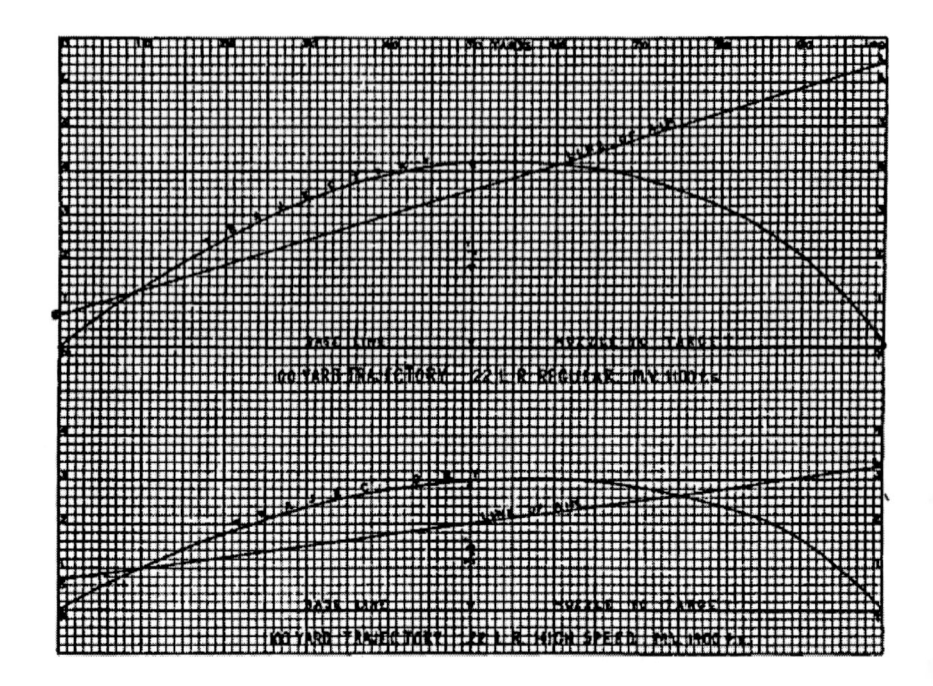

PLATE 23

Similarly for the high-speed cartridge, if you set your sights for 75 yards your bullet will strike 1 inch high at 40 yards, drop about 1 inch low at 85 yards, 1 1/3 inches low at 90 yards, and 3 1/3 inches low at 100 yards. Aiming directly at an object you will not miss your point of aim by more than an inch from the muzzle to 85 yards.

In field shooting it is usually much more practical to set the sights in some such manner, and then allow for the rise or fall of the bullet, than to set the sights for the estimated distance, because you very often have to estimate the distance quickly and fire at once, and you have no time to set sights. You see a target appear, you estimate it to be 80 yards, you are using regular velocity ammunition, so you hold two inches high to allow for the drop of the bullet. The reason why we set our sights for 60 and 75 yards in the two foregoing examples is because these settings give us the longest distance with regular and high-speed ammunition at which our bullets will not miss the point of aim by more than an inch.

ESTIMATING DISTANCE

You should practice estimating distances until you become skilled at it. Measure off 100 yards over a piece of ground. Set up a natural target of known size, or a three-inch "Splat" target, or any other object. Note how it appears at various distances on your 100-yard course. Aim at it at various distances and see how much of it is covered by the width of your front sight.

Set up a standard 100-yard target at 100 yards, with 6-inch aiming bull's-eye, and aim at it steadily. How much in width on the target does the top of your front sight cover? If it seems to be exactly as wide as the bull's-eye, then you can say your front sight subtends 6 inches at 100 yards, or 3 inches at 50 yards. If you then were to aim at a 3-inch target, and it appeared just the width of your front sight, it would then be approximately 50 yards away—say between 40 and 60 yards, because you cannot measure accurately enough with your eye to see the small difference that 10 yards would make in the subtended angle.

Such practice, also regular shooting on the 50 and 100-yards small bore range, will soon accustom you to how things look at various distances, to how they compare with the width of your front sight, and to the extent of ground between you and the object, so that soon you can estimate the distance to any object quite closely. It is also profitable to continue this practice beyond 100 yards, although this distance is about the limit of effective field shooting at small objects with the small bore rifle.

RULES

There are no established rules for field shooting, except that safety precautions must be observed. Every shooter or club makes rules to suit the occasion. It is usually best to make no rules restricting the shooter or his rifle, but to make the game more difficult or interesting, as skill is acquired, by varying the target or the time, shooting at more difficult targets or in a shorter time limit. The object is to learn to hit small, rather indistinct targets at long, unknown distances with the greatest speed. Competitions can be arranged in any way desired. Who can make the greatest number of hits in the fewest shots? Who can hit all the targets in the fewest shots? Who can break all the targets in the shortest time?

SAFETY

Field firing targets should be set up only in front of a hill or other backstop which will stop the bullets. They can be set up on a regular small bore rifle range, although this would have the disadvantage of permitting the shooters to know the distance to the targets. Stony ground should be avoided as bullets would glance from it and possibly fly over the bullet stop. Bullets do not glance from dry sand, and seldom from loam covered with grass. Remember that the extreme range of the .22 Long Rifle cartridge is 1,500 yards with barrel elevated at an angle of 30 degrees. A ricochet may fly as far as 500 yards from the spot from which it glances. Bullets are dangerous at these extreme ranges.

CHAPTER XI

CARE OF THE RIFLE

A .22 caliber rifle needs daily cleaning and attention when in use, and proper storage when not in use, or its accuracy and effectiveness will deteriorate rapidly; but, if properly taken care of, a good rifle will last you a lifetime, as it practically never wears out from firing alone.

You should understand clearly the effect of rust. Many people think that rust can be removed. Red rust is evidence of the eating away of the surface of the metal. Even if you remove the red evidence you can never repair the damage the rusting has caused. Rust is always the result of neglect or ignorance. A clean steel surface oiled to protect from moisture does not rust. Never allow even a suspicion of rust to appear on or in your rifle. It will not appear if you will care for your rifle as described below.

Many shooters complain that their barrel "leads", that it gets full of lead and will not shoot accurately. A .22 caliber rifle barrel that is properly used will not lead if rightly cared for, no lead being deposited in the bore that cannot be pushed out at once with a snug-fitting flannel cleaning patch. But a barrel that has been permitted to rust slightly will have a rough, pitted bore, and such a barrel may lead. There is no cure for this except a new barrel to replace the one you have ruined by neglect. An automatic rifle may lead or "copper" if fired very rapidly for a large number of rounds. Instructions for removing such lead or coppering are given below.

You should understand the action of the fouling of the various types of .22 Long Rifle cartridges. The particular priming, powder, and bullets with which a cartridge is loaded are always given on the pasteboard carton in which the cartridges are packed.

Cartridges loaded with non-corrosive priming, smokeless powder, and lubricated or film coated lead bullets leave a fouling in the bore which is both non-corrosive and rust preventative. It is very easy to keep the bore in condition when such ammunition is used. Ordinarily, if this type of cartridge is used exclusively the bore need not be cleaned from day to day while the rifle is in continued use, although there is no objection to cleaning it. But the bore should be cleaned when putting the rifle away for a long period, or in localities where the air is excessively damp.

Cartridges loaded with non-corrosive priming, smokeless powder, and copper or cadmium-plated bullets give a non-corrosive but not a rust-preventing fouling. On rare occasions after such cartridges have been fired the bore might rust from moisture in the air, particularly damp night air. It is therefore safest to clean the bore not later than the evening of the day on which it was fired.

Some target varieties of cartridges are loaded with Lesmok or Semi-smokeless powder because of the superior accuracy of such powders. The fouling of these powders will cause rust if the bore be not properly cared for. When such ammunition is used the bore should *always* be cleaned as described below not later than the evening of the day on which the rifle was fired, then no deterioration of the bore will occur. If the rifle be left overnight without cleaning rust will start.

Ordinarily fouling does not accumulate in a good barrel during a day's firing to an extent that would interfere with accuracy unless the atmosphere is very hot and devoid of moisture, when cleaning between strings is recommended. Therefore, there is no advantage in cleaning in the middle of the day's firing or between scores. Clean before evening when the air becomes damp.

PLATE 24 Tip of Cleaning Rod

Never use .22 Short cartridges in a rifle chambered for the .22 Long Rifle cartridge. Gas will escape just in front of the mouth of the short case and erode the chamber, and eventually this erosion will ruin the barrel.

For cleaning you need a steel cleaning rod with a tip like that shown in Plate 24, a supply of canton flannel cleaning patches, and a can of gun oil. Patches should be cut from a medium weight canton flannel, about three-quarters inch square, so that when centered with the tip of the cleaning rod and pushed into the bore, they will make a snug fit in the bore, but not so tight that the patch might be punctured by the rod, or that the rod and patch might get stuck in the bore. Clean from the breech of the barrel if possible, but if the mechanism of the rifle will not permit this, then clean from the muzzle and use fingers as a guide to prevent the cleaning rod rubbing and wearing the muzzle.

1. Wet a flannel patch with water, powder solvent, or light oil, lay it over the breech or muzzle, center it with the tip of the cleaning rod, and push it straight through the bore and out the other end. This pushes out the bulk of the fouling.

2. Swab the bore with two or three patches wet with water, powder solvent, or light oil. To swab: Place a piece of paper on the floor, rest the muzzle on it, push the patch down to the paper, and pull it back to the chamber a dozen times, thus swabbing the bore thoroughly from end to end with each patch.

3. Dry the rod. Then swab again with about half a dozen clean, dry patches so that the bore is thoroughly dried and cleaned out, and becomes slightly warm from friction.

4. Saturate a patch with gun oil and swab the bore with it, and leave the bore in this condition. The bore is now clean and protected and will not rust. If you are putting the rifle away for over a week, the next day wipe out the oil and swab with a patch heavily coated with gun grease. Do not use "powder solvent" for this last swabbing. It is a cleaner only, and not a good rust preventative.

5. Wipe the exterior of the rifle and all parts of the mechanism that can be reached with a dry rag and then with an oily one.

6. Before starting to fire always push a clean, dry patch through the bore to wipe out the film of oil or grease. Oil in the bore and chamber will cause the first few shots to fly slightly wild until the oil is shot out. Grease in the bore may cause serious injury to the barrel if the rifle be fired without removing it. Gasoline on a patch will facilitate the removal of grease.

Sometimes an automatic rifle that is fired very rapidly for some time, so that the barrel gets very hot, will have lead or copper deposited in the bore. To remove this, screw a brass bristle brush on the rod, dip the brush in kerosene, and swab the bore with it, pushing the brush all the way through the bore, and then pulling it all the way back, without reversing it in the bore.

The above cleaning is all that is necessary to preserve the rifle in first-class condition indefinitely. It is the one best way. Other methods may or may not be efficient. Note also the following:

The bolt, particularly its interior mechanism, should merely be wiped dry and then wiped with a slightly oily rag. Any quantity of oil or grease on the interior mechanism of a bolt may cause poor accuracy by interfering with perfect ignition.

On a sandy or dusty range pay particular attention to

keeping the action clean during use. The cutting effect of sand or dust on the moving parts may cause wear which would eventually result in the rifle not breeching up tight enough for accuracy or safety.

Perspiration is a great promoter of rust, so after use, wipe the exterior of the rifle with a dry rag and then with an oily one. Occasionally rub raw linseed oil into the stock, and neatsfoot oil into the gunsling. Do not lay the rifle on damp ground or grass as it might warp the stock—use your forked rifle rest. After a rifle has been wet from rain wipe it off dry, oil the metal parts, and apply linseed oil to the stock. Constantly guard the rifle and its sights against blows and falls.

CHAPTER XII

SMALL BORE TARGETS

The official targets used in small bore rifle shooting are printed on unfinished tag board for shooting at 50 and 75 ft. indoors and 50, 100 and 200 yards and 50 meters outdoors.

The targets used at 50 and 75 ft. indoors, and dimensions, are shown in Plate 25. The 6 to 10 rings are blackened to give the black aiming bull's-eye. These indoor targets are usually printed with either 5 or 10 targets on one cardboard sheet measuring approximately 10 3/4 × 13 inches. Where 10 bull's-eyes are shown, the shooter fires only one shot at each of them; where 5 bull's-eyes are used, he fires two shots in succession at each of the 5 bull's-eyes. Accurate scoring makes it necessary to fire no more than two shots at any one target because at these ranges a group of ten shots fired on one target would probably cut one large hole through the center of the bull's-eye and it would be impossible to tell which of the shots were 8's, 9's or 10's.

DIMENSIONS

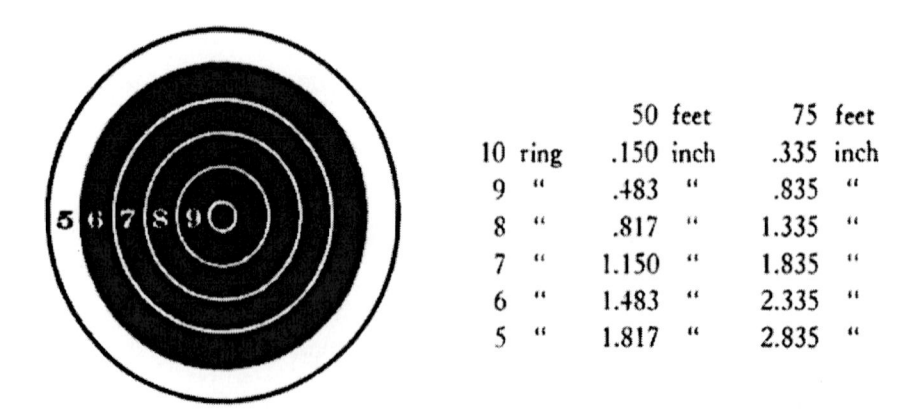

	50 feet	75 feet
10 ring	.150 inch	.335 inch
9 "	.483 "	.835 "
8 "	.817 "	1.335 "
7 "	1.150 "	1.835 "
6 "	1.483 "	2.335 "
5 "	1.817 "	2.835 "

PLATE 25—Standard N. R. A. Indoor Target, 50 Feet or 75 Feet

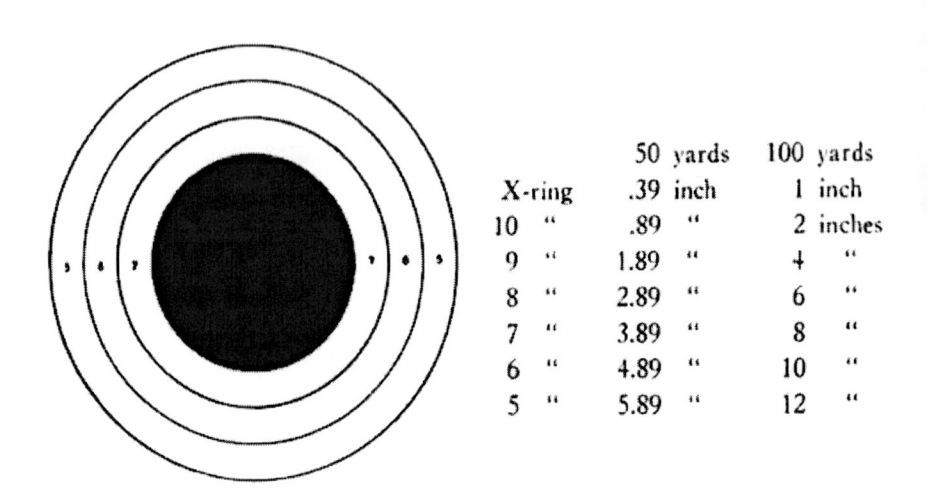

	50 yards	100 yards
X-ring	.39 inch	1 inch
10 "	.89 "	2 inches
9 "	1.89 "	4 "
8 "	2.89 "	6 "
7 "	3.89 "	8 "
6 "	4.89 "	10 "
5 "	5.89 "	12 "

PLATE 26A—Standard N. R. A. 50 and 100-Yard Target

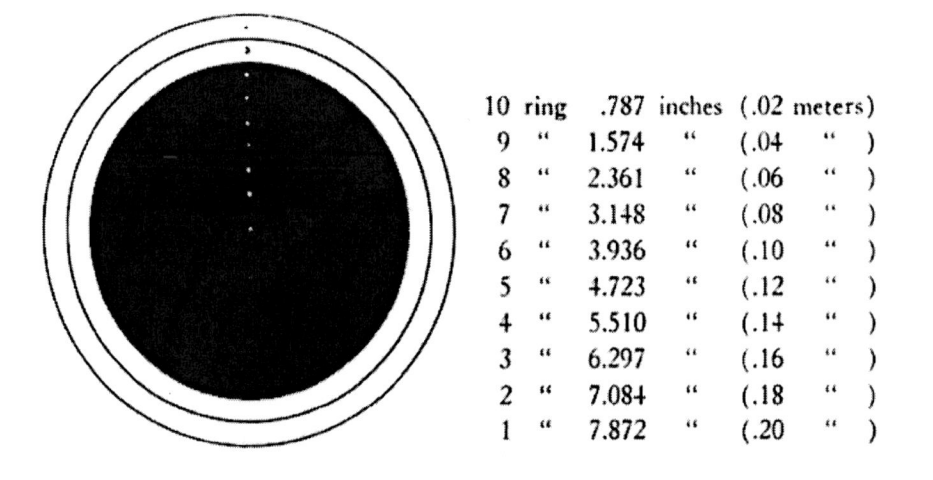

10 ring	.787 inches	(.02 meters)
9 "	1.574 "	(.04 ")
8 "	2.361 "	(.06 ")
7 "	3.148 "	(.08 ")
6 "	3.936 "	(.10 ")
5 "	4.723 "	(.12 ")
4 "	5.510 "	(.14 ")
3 "	6.297 "	(.16 ")
2 "	7.084 "	(.18 ")
1 "	7.872 "	(.20 ")

PLATE 26B—Standard N. R. A. 50 Meter Target

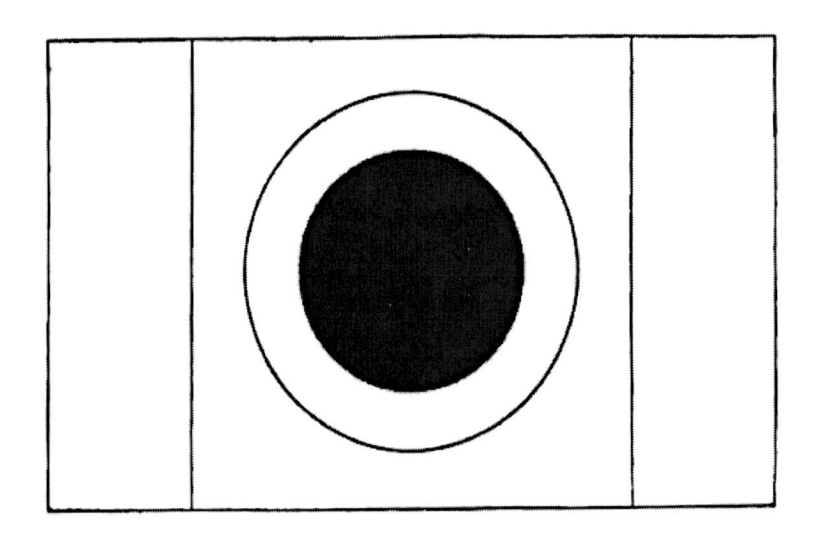

PLATE 27—The C-5 Target for 150, 175, and 200 Yards

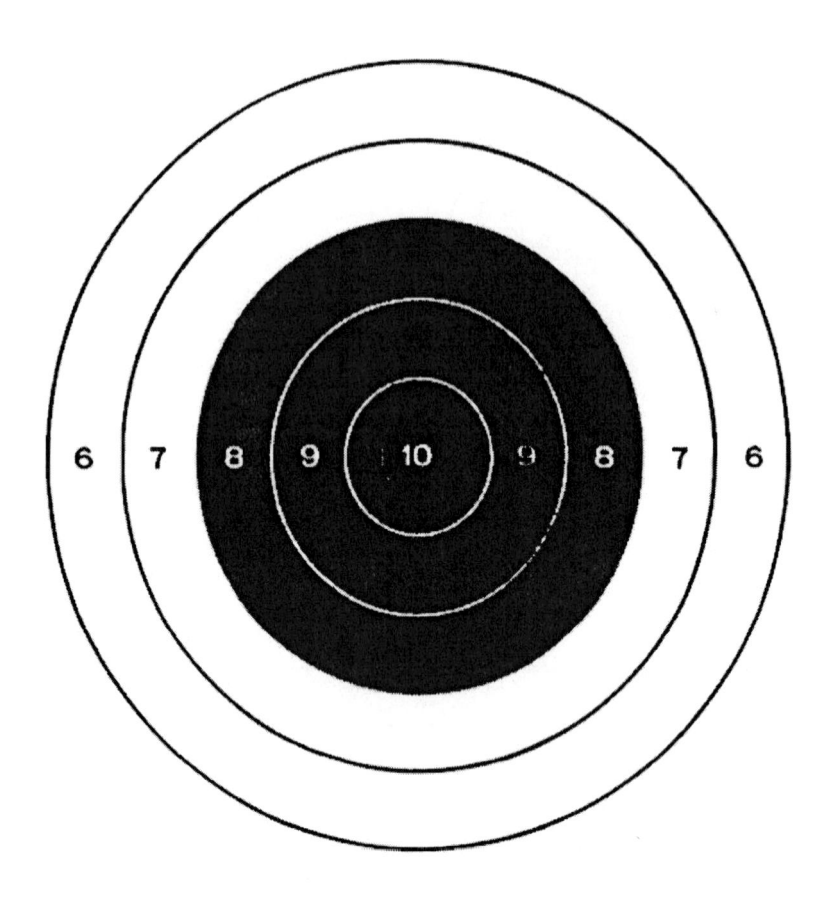

PLATE 28

The targets used at 50 and 100 yards outdoors have dimensions as shown in the table opposite Plate 26A. The 8, 9 and 10 rings are blackened to give the black aiming bull's-eye. Sometimes in important matches two targets are set up alongside of each other, or two targets are printed on one cardboard, 5 shots being fired at each target to facilitate accurate scoring of each shot. More recently in registered N. R. A. matches, it has been customary to print two or four bull's-eyes on one target card and these bull's-eyes are numbered to establish the order of fire in the ranking of tied scores.

For some years, the official target for 200-yard shooting has been one known as the "Decimal" target, which is illustrated in Plate 28. The 8, 9 and 10 rings are blackened to give the black aiming bull's-eye. This target is printed on thin cardboard sheets and is used exclusively at 200 yards. The dimensions are:

X-ring	2 inches	8 ring	12 inches
10 "	4 "	7 "	16 "
9 "	8 "	6 "	20 "

Size of cardboard 21" × 24"

In addition to the 200-yard decimal targets, there is another target which is sometimes used for long range small bore shooting at 150, 175 and 200 yards, known as the C-5 Target. This is illustrated in Plate 27. It gets its name from the fact that it is a reduction of the Army Target "C", used at 800, 900 and 1,000 yards with the .30 Caliber Springfield Military Rifle, but is reduced to one-fifth size. It is printed on a thin cardboard sheet 15 inches × 24 1/2 inches. The black bull's-eye counting 5 is 7.2 inches in diameter with a V-ring of 4 inches. The 4-ring is 10.6 inches in diameter. The space counting 3 is a square in the center of the target 14.4 inches on each side. The spaces counting 2 at each end of the target are 4.8 inches × 14.4 inches, which makes the entire counting target 14.4 inches × 24 inches.

Small Bore Matches are often shot at 50 meters (54.6 yards) under International Shooting Union and Olympic conditions. The 50-meter target is similar to the 300-meter International Free-Rifle target, reduced to one-sixth size and has the dimensions as shown in the table opposite Plate 26B. The 4 to 10 rings are blackened to form a sighting bull.

Matches at 50 meters have become very popular in recent years since this target rewards very close holding, and it is the target which is used in several of the International team matches.

CHAPTER XIII

SMALL BORE RIFLE RANGES

It is, of course, apparent that if a shooter or a newly organized rifle club is to undertake small bore rifle shooting, a suitable indoor or outdoor rifle range is necessary. Often great difficulty is experienced in obtaining such a range, although usually one can be had if some energy and ingenuity are exercised to obtain it. Once a location has been found the matter of proper equipment is comparatively easy, and not necessarily expensive.

Often a range is already in existence in your locality. A letter addressed to The Secretary, National Rifle Association, 1600 Rhode Island Ave., Washington, D. C., will bring information as to the nearest civilian rifle clubs to your locality, and these clubs usually have ranges. National Guard armories sometimes open their ranges for use by civilian shooters on certain evenings or days. Similar shooting arrangements can sometimes be made at the nearest Army Post.

In towns and small cities a suitable location for an outdoor range can almost always be found on a nearby farm. Farmers are usually willing to rent the necessary ground for a very reasonable figure as very little ground is needed, merely enough for the firing points and butts, with paths leading thereto, the remainder of the ground shot over being planted in low crops. Also a farmer may even donate the ground because of ability to sell some of the produce of his farm to members of a rifle club, or he may become interested in rifle shooting himself. Of course the ground must be suitable and safe. Instructions for selecting suitable and safe ground will be found in this chapter.

Even in large cities the obtaining of a range is not always as difficult as it would seem. On a recent afternoon's survey in a large city the writer found a vacant lot with a high brick wall on its North side, two basements, and the flat roof of a garage, all of which could be obtained for a reasonable rental. With safe backstops and bulkheads any of these localities could have been made into a suitable small bore range. When a club is organized among the employees of a large industrial organization that organization can often find a suitable location on its premises.

Small bore rifle ranges, due to difference in construction surroundings, and location, may be divided into Indoor Gallery Ranges at 50 and 75 feet, Outdoor Ranges at 50 feet and 50 and 100 yards, and Long Ranges at 150, 175 and 200 yards. The exact distances are important because these are the ranges at which all small bore shooting competitions are held in the United States. England, Canada, and all British

Colonies also use the 50 and 100-yard ranges with targets exactly similar to ours. The great advantage of these ranges is that they can almost always be conveniently located in or very close to towns or cities where they are easily accessible to all who desire to shoot on them. It is easy and relatively cheap to build them so that they are perfectly safe. The members of a club, or even an individual rifleman, can build perfectly satisfactory ranges in their spare time, sometimes at practically no cost. Indoor gallery ranges can be located in cellars, basements, gymnasiums, or any place indoors where there is sufficient room. Outdoor ranges for 50 and 100 yards can be constructed so that they can be safely located in a city park or in a vacant lot. The report of a small bore rifle is so slight that no objection by the surrounding residents will be encountered if proper safety precautions are taken.

JUNIOR RIFLE RANGES

Small bore rifle shooting has become quite popular in all types of educational institutions from the grammar up to and including the high schools and colleges, also among the Boy Scouts and in boys' and girls' Summer camps. It is a simple matter to set up a satisfactory and safe indoor and outdoor range by following the rules laid down elsewhere in this book. The standard distance for junior shooting is 50 feet, and on account of this short range a suitable location with a natural hillside backstop may be easily obtained. The National Rifle

Association of America, 1600 Rhode Island Ave., Washington, D. C., conducts a Junior Department of Shooting for boys and girls below the age of 19 years and will gladly furnish complete information on application covering formation of rifle clubs, building of ranges, rules and regulations regarding competitions, as well as how to become an N. R. A. Jr. Marksman.

SAFETY PRECAUTIONS

The designs for small bore ranges which follow are predicated on the assumption that a certain amount of necessary discipline will be enforced on those who use these ranges, and that common sense precautions will be taken. No rifle range will ever be safe for the idiot who points his rifle, loaded or unloaded, at another; who fires his rifle in the air or to the rear, or who proceeds to fire without being familiar with the operation and loading of his weapon. Rifles must be kept unloaded and the breech actions open until the firer is in shooting position at the firing point, with his rifle pointed towards the target. No man must go forward from the firing point to inspect or change the targets until everyone at the firing point has unloaded his rifle, and laid his rifle down with the breech action open.

Small bore rifles using the .22 caliber Long Rifle cartridge have an extreme range of about 1,500 yards when the barrel is elevated at an angle of about 33 degrees. Even at this extreme range the little bullet has remaining energy and penetration sufficient to seriously wound a human being. At short ranges the following thicknesses of material have been found to be proof against occasional direct hits:

12 inches of earth or sand
3 inches of gravel between planks
4 1/2 inches concrete or good brickwork
5 inches of hard timber, such as railroad ties, etc.
6 inches of fine gravel
1/8 inch steel plate

Where continuous direct hits are to be expected, as immediately behind the paper targets, double the above protection is necessary, but as the bullets will gradually wear away most of the above materials and thus gradually drive through, it is most economical and convenient to use a 1/4-inch steel plate or similar thickness of boiler iron, preferably set at an angle of 45 degrees so the bullets will be deflected downward into a box of sand. In positions where only occasional glancing hits may be expected, such as side walls, floors, or ceilings, the following thicknesses may be considered to be safe:

1 inch planking
Ordinary plaster
Galvanized iron roofing
Tile or slate roof.

INDOOR GALLERY RANGES

Such ranges can be constructed in almost any cellar, basement, gymnasium, or other large room where there is sufficient space. The range is measured from the firing point to the target so the room should be at least 15 feet longer than the range to give room for targets, backstop, men lying at the firing point, and room to move back and forth behind the firing point. The room should be capable of ventilation, should have electric light wiring installed, and, if there are any doors or windows in the line of fire, they should be blocked off, closed, and protected by material impervious to bullets, as noted above.

A very simple combined backstop, target carrier and light may be made. It consists of a box backed by a 1/4-inch steel plate set at an angle of 45 degrees. The back is a steel plate which deflects the bullets downward, the bottom of the box being filled with about 3 inches of sand to catch the bullets. The front boards, on which the paper gallery target is fastened with thumbtacks, slide in slots at the front corners of the box, and are removable so that they can be replaced as they are shot away. The framework of the box should be made of 2 × 4-inch lumber, with 7/8-inch boards for the remainder. A 2 × 6-inch board faced with white paper to reflect light is used with a 60-watt Mazda globe, the board being placed at an angle to best reflect light over the surface of the target.

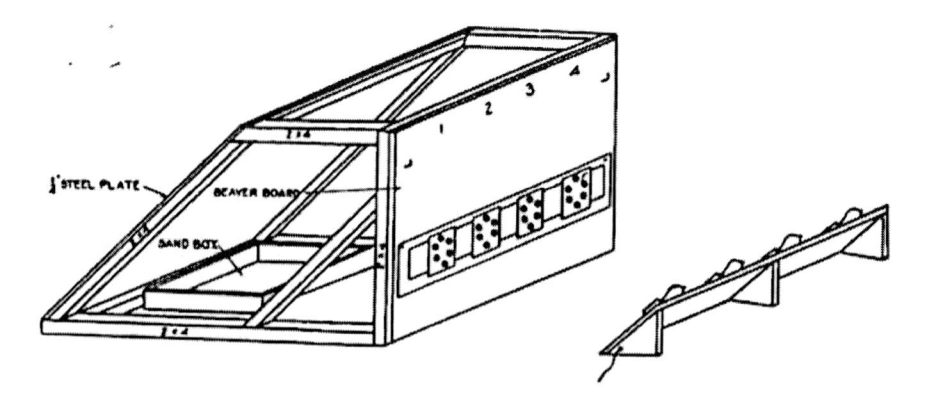

PLATE 29—Simple Arrangement of Backstop, Targets, and Lights for a Club Gallery

The cellar or room should be dark, except for the light at the target, and, if desired, a light behind the shooter. The box is placed on the floor for prone shooting, or on a pair of wooden horses for standing. This arrangement works very well if one to three fairly skilled and careful riflemen only are using the gallery. But, if a club is to use this arrangement, there should be some sort of a backstop immediately behind the target box to catch the occasional wild shots. This backstop should be at least 5 feet high and 6 feet wide for each target. It might consist of 1/8-inch steel plate, or a pile of railroad ties, or a bulkhead of double board 4 inches apart with fine gravel filled in behind the boards. It may also be desirable to face the lamp board with 1/8-inch steel plate or boiler iron to prevent a stray shot damaging the light. In a club gallery there should be some kind of a fence just in front of the firing point to prevent anyone straying into the danger zone in front of the rifles. This fence should have a gate with an electric switch so that, when anyone opens the gate and goes forward to tack up a fresh target, the light at the target will go out automatically. When the light goes out everyone at the firing point should at once open the breech of his rifle and leave it open until the light goes on. Telescopes or field glasses at the firing point permit the shooter to see where each of his shots strikes.

Plate 29 shows a similar arrangement, but much larger and more suitable for a large club gallery or for use in a gymnasium or armory. The unit permits of four men firing at one time, each man having his own target. It consists of a framework of 2 × 4-inch lumber, faced with a sheet of beaver board, and backed by a 1/4-inch steel plate set at an angle of 45 degrees to deflect the bullets downward into a sand box. The front of the framework should be about 5 feet high by 9 feet long. The beaver board front is replaced when large holes have been shot in it. One unit is placed opposite the center of four firing points, and as many units as required may be used. In an armory or gymnasium the units may be raised with crowbars, rollers slipped under them, and they can then be run off to one side when not in use, or they may be constructed on wheels. To lighten them for moving around, the sand box may be made as a separate tray and slipped under them. Racks containing four targets, as described below for the 50 and 100-

yard outdoor ranges, are hung in front of the beaver board on pins, the targets being tacked to the racks about a foot apart. Two racks are provided, and, while one rack is being fired upon, the other one is having fresh targets tacked on it for the next relay of shooters. After a relay completes its scores, rifles are unloaded and breech actions opened by command, the lights at the targets are turned off, and a man takes down the new rack of targets, hangs it up and brings back the old rack for scoring. For prone shooting the rack is hung about two feet from the floor, and, for standing shooting, about four feet from the floor.

PLATE 30

Lights may be arranged for as shown in the plate by placing a board on the floor about five feet in front of the targets, with white paper tacked on its face, and carrying strong Mazda lamps. This lamp board can be removed when not in use. Or a hanging frame may be arranged to suspend the lights about 5 or 6 feet above the floor and in front of the targets. With this overhead lighting a very satisfactory light can be secured by using two General Electric Co. Type L-9, 500-watt Flood Lights with stippled lenses, placing the lights about 15 feet in front of the targets and directing the lamps at a mid-point between the upper and the lower positions of the targets.

PLATE 31—X-Ring Centrifugal Bullet Trap

Another more durable and elaborate unit is that known as the "X-ring Centrifugal Bullet Trap". It consists of a steel, funnel-shaped box, the funnel guiding the bullets into an inner scroll where their energy is dissipated by friction and centrifugal action. The box is supported in position by a standard. The paper target is secured by convenient clamps at the opening of the funnel, and suitable electric light fixtures are provided. Plate 31 illustrates this unit which has proved very practical. An individual can set one up in the basement of his home and have a very satisfactory range in a few minutes, or any number of units may be set up side by side on a larger range.

The above units are all that are necessary if only fairly good, careful shots are to use the gallery; but, if uninstructed or careless men are to use it, some backstop must be placed in rear of the units as described above, or it may even be necessary to place a bullet-proof bulkhead a short distance in front of the firing points, as described below, for the protected outdoor range, to surely catch any bullets which would not strike the steel plate of the unit.

One-quarter inch steel plates, or similar boiler iron, inclined at an angle of 45 degrees to deflect the bullets downward into a sand box, are by far the best and most durable arrangement to catch the bullets behind the targets. The objection to placing this plate vertical is that the bullets splash backward objectionably. If the plate cannot be obtained, some arrangement such as railroad ties, or frames filled with fine gravel, may be used instead, but these must be inspected frequently and replaced when necessary, as the bullets will gradually drill holes through them immediately in rear of each target.

At the firing point the positions from which each shooter fires should be arranged at least four feet apart, five feet if possible. They should be marked by a plain number painted on the floor, or a short stake bearing the number, and a similar plain number should be painted above the corresponding target's position on the backstop, as shown on Plate 29. Firing points should also be provided with some sort of mat which will cushion the elbows from the hard floor. Gymnasium mats are the best, but expensive; ordinary door mats will do.

Much more elaborate and convenient gallery ranges may be constructed, if desired. Permanently constructed steel bullet stops and flood lights are installed. The targets are suspended from carriers which run on wires suspended from the ceiling and running from the firing point to the bullet stop. The shooter at the firing point affixes a target in the carrier, and turns a wheel which runs the target down to the firing position, thus making it unnecessary for anyone to go forward of the firing point, and also permitting any one shooter to change his target at any time he desires, or reel it back to the firing point for inspection without the other shooters having to stop firing. Complete plans and blue prints for the construction of permanent ranges of this kind may be obtained from The Secretary, National Rifle Association, 1600 Rhode Island Ave., Washington, D. C. Also see Plate 30 illustrating such a range.

OUTDOOR RANGES

Outdoor shooting with small bore rifles is, as a rule, more interesting than gallery shooting, and one learns more. Outdoor shooting can be carried on at all periods during the year when the weather is not too cold. Indeed it can be carried on all year if a warm shooting house with ports to shoot from can be afforded. Even moderate rain need not deter the enthusiast if there is a cheap roof shelter over the firing point. They may even be used at night by illuminating the targets with electric flood lights, as described for the gallery range. The only problem of the outdoor range is to secure a suitable location. It is sometimes possible to obtain a large vacant lot in a town or city which will be very convenient and easily reached, and ranges have often been built in out of the way corners in city parks. Usually, however, one will have to go a short distance out into the country to build the range, preferably to a location that can easily be reached by trolley or automobile.

The discussion of outdoor ranges from this point on will be divided into two classes: (1) Ranges in not too well built up areas where there is either a large, adequate, natural backstop such as a hill 40 feet to 50 feet high and of a slope not less than three to two or a clear area appproximately 50 yards wide and 1,400 yards deep from the firing point, that can be adequately observed, into which the bullet may fall; and (2) Safety ranges for use in public parks and closely built up areas where safety facilities are provided to prevent bullets fired in the direction of the target from missing the backstop.

In any case, the site should be fairly level or at least the firing point and the targets should be level. The lot should be at least 110 yards long, and wide enough to accommodate the number of firing points desired, with preferably at least 25 yards to spare on each side of the range proper. If a piece of ground can be obtained which is at least 220 yards long, that would be ideal, as this would permit installing a 200-yard range, but the 200-yard range is by no means essential for the thorough enjoyment of the small bore game. The range should face preferably north, northeast, or east, so the sun will not be in the eyes of the shooters at the time of day they use the range most, and so that the targets will not be in the shade.

Firing Points, Targets and Backstop of Modern Safety Range, Union County Park, Elizabeth, N. J.

It is necessary that there be some sort of a backstop to catch the bullets and that this be sufficiently large to stop the occasional slightly wild shot that goes wide of the targets. No range is safe with the careless man who discharges his rifle to the rear or pointed upward, and we must always depend on a certain discipline being exercised on a rifle range and certain safety precautions being rigidly enforced. If possible, there should be a steep hill behind the targets, extending at least 15 to 20 feet above the line of fire. If the hill be not steep, it should be kept ploughed up to prevent bullets glancing and carrying on to places where they would be dangerous. Beware particularly of a hill composed largely of rock or gravel. If there be no hill, then an artificial backstop should be built in rear of the targets extending, if possible, 6 feet above the line of targets and 6 feet beyond the flank targets. On a city lot a brick wall or a brick or stone building might sometimes provide a sufficient backstop for the very wild shots, but in such case there should be a built-up backstop immediately behind the targets which will catch 99 per cent of the shots and keep them from gradually drilling into the wall. Such built-up backstops can consist of piles of logs or railroad ties, or two rough board walls filled in with a foot thickness of earth between, or, if fine gravel can be had, six inches thickness will suffice.

For use in public parks where all safety precautions must be taken, the Institute has prepared a design for a 50-yard and

100-yard small bore rifle range in which the rifle is fired with the muzzle inserted in one end of an 8-foot length of 8-inch iron pipe. The bullet passes through a port in a bulkhead placed 20 feet ahead of the firing point and is stopped by a large backstop placed 5 feet to 10 feet beyond the 100-yard target point. This design has been so arranged that all bullets fired into the pipe will strike either the bullet catcher at 20 feet or the backstop behind the 100-yard point. In the design, the iron pipes are placed so that they are level and approximately 3 feet above the natural ground level and at the same height as the targets. This has several advantages: it makes necessary a somewhat elevated firing point that will drain quickly and it will reduce frequent mowing of the grass between the firing point and target. If this design is carefully followed, even the accidental discharge of the gun into the tube which might ricochet two or more times from the walls of the tube will be caught by the bullet catcher. Examination of the design will show that the bullet catcher consists of two layers of material; 1-inch board facing on the side toward the firing point and 1/8-inch steel facing on the side toward the target. This board facing is highly desirable, otherwise bullet splash from the steel might throw back to the firing point, causing eye injuries.

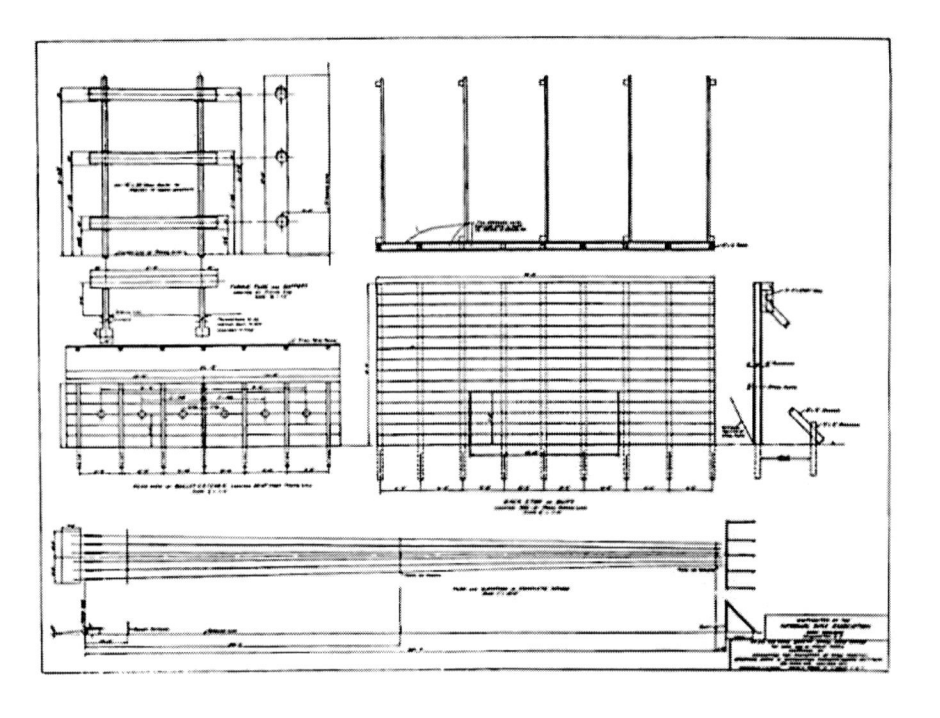

Working Plans, 50 and 100-Yard Small Bore Safely Range

If no other provision is made except the iron pipes, an adequate backstop would have to be 25 feet above the center line of the targets plus some reasonable safety factor. With the bullet catcher at 20 feet ahead of the firing point, a backstop 10 feet above the center line of the targets plus a 2-foot safety factor should be adequate. This backstop must extend to the right and left of the targets approximately the same distance.

The design which has been prepared by the Institute is for a six-target range which can be used either for six targets at 50 yards, or six targets at 100 yards, or three at 50 yards and three at 100 yards. If it is desired to build a larger range than this (for instance, a 12-target range), it would not be necessary to build a backstop twice as long as the present one. If the second group of targets were placed close to the first group, then the backstop would only have to be increased in length by the space occupied by the additional targets.

The following list of material has been prepared for such a six-target range.

50 AND 100-YARD SAFETY SMALL BORE RANGE

Firing Point (24' long, 7' wide, 22" high at front, 10" at rear)
Approx. 8 cu. yd.
6 pc. 8" W. I. Pipe 8 ft. long
24 Hook Bolts
Concrete supports for same (3.5 cu. yd.)

Bullet Catcher (Safety Stop)
7 pc. 4" x 4" x 8'   } Creosoted
6 pc. 1" x 12" x 26' } Lumber
156 sq. ft. ½" sheet iron, 788 lbs.
Cutting 6 holes in sheet iron

Target Frames—4 needed (17" x 6')
Stop Butt (15' high x 32' long)
9 pc. 6" x 6" x 18'
1 pc. 6" x 6" x 10'
60 pcs. 1½" x 12" x 16'   } Creosoted
*1 pc. 6" x 6" x 10'   } Lumber
*1 pc. 6" x 6" x 16'
*5 pc. 3" x 8" x 24'

Cracked Rock & Chat for Filling
15 tons
2 pc. ¾" thick steel 5' x 7'

If terrain permits placing targets near natural butt, a hill at least twenty-five feet high with a slope not less than 3/2 and with *no* exposed rock, the largest item of cost is eliminated.

---
* Wind bracing.

It should be noted that of the total cost about 35 per cent is labor, which may well be performed by the members of a club with proportional saving. It should also be noted that of the total expense of the range, well over half of it is represented in the cost of the backstop. Care in selecting a location, which will permit the placing of the targets near the base of a hill with a slope of not less than three to two and with no exposed rock, will eliminate this larger item of cost.

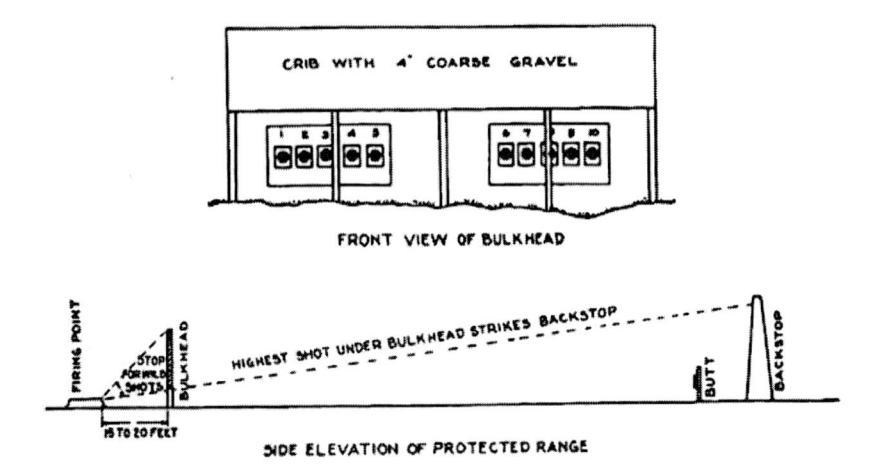

PLATE 32—Fence or Butt for Hanging the Target Racks on Protected Range With Bulkhead

If the range is built in a public park, it should be fenced along the line 30 feet or 40 feet to either side of the center line of the range to prevent children from running into the line of fire.

Complete blueprints and working drawings for such a range can be obtained from the National Rifle Association, 1600 Rhode Island Ave., Washington, D. C.

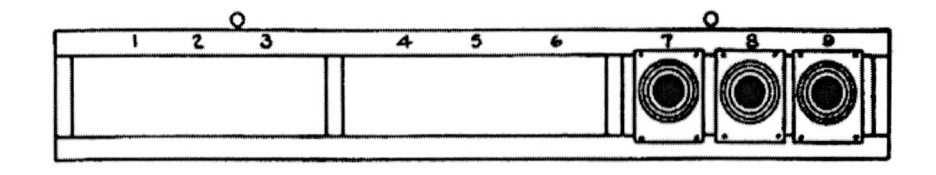

PLATE 33—Racks for Outdoor Targets

Targets are easily arranged for outdoor ranges of 50 feet, 50 and 100 yards. A rough board fence should be erected in front of the backstop and the correct distance (50 feet, 50 and 100 yards) in front of the firing point. This fence should be about six feet high and built with 2 × 4 uprights faced with rough boards. It is most convenient and economical to build the fence in sections about 15 feet long for the various distances. These sections should be placed opposite the center of each 5 firing points, the targets for five men (three targets for each man may sometimes be needed) being tacked on racks and the racks hung on these fences. The slight convergence of the fire of five men on such a butt does no harm. Such a fence or butt is shown in Plate 32. There should be an open gap in the fence immediately behind the bull's-eyes of the targets as they hang in the racks, this being obtained by leaving one board out of the fence. This gap is to permit light to shine through the targets from the rear, thus making the bullet holes in the black bull's-eye plainly visible when viewed from the firing point through the shooter's spotting telescope. (See Chapter

I, "Accessories".) At the top of the fence, above each target or series of three targets, should be painted a large white number corresponding to the number of the firing point, and showing the shooter which are his targets. The remainder of the fence should be painted dark green.

Model Target Frame [Double Target System]

The targets are tacked on rectangular racks of boards made of wood strips about 3 inches wide, as shown in Plate 33, long enough to hold five to nine targets tacked alongside of one another, with about 1 inch between targets. Two sets of racks are provided for each butt. One set, with the targets tacked on, is taken down and hung up in position on the butt or fence, as shown in Plate 32, and five men at the firing point fire their scores on these targets. When these shooters complete their firing, a man takes down a set of new racks, hangs them up in place of the old ones, and brings the old ones back behind the firing point for scoring and record. As a safety precaution it is absolutely essential that the official at the firing point give the command for all shooters at the firing point to unload their rifles, open chambers, and lay the rifles down before a man goes forward to change target racks.

Because small bore rifle matches at ranges of 100 yards and less are fired without each shot being scored and posted as fired, it has been necessary to devise a double target system which is now required in all National and Registered competitions recognized by the National Rifle Association.

The targets are held in double racks constructed similarly to those shown in Plate 34. The "record target" carrying the bull's-eyes is placed in the front and the "backing target," which is a plain card without bull's-eyes, is placed on the rear. The proper interval is shown in the accompanying table. In competition the target card carries one bull's-eye for sighting shots and two or more bull's-eyes (depending on the conditions of the match) for the record shots. The target cards are usually tacked or clipped onto a piece of composition board with holes properly spaced behind each bull's-eye so that the light may come through from the rear and assist in spotting the shots. The composition board is fastened to the frames with turnbuttons or in some other quickly detachable manner.

Distance Between Firing Points	Distance Between Targets	
	100 Yards	50 Yards
4 feet	18¾"	9⅜"
4 feet, 6 inches	16⅝"	8⅛"
5 feet	15"	7½"
5 feet, 6 inches	13⅜"	6⅞"
6 feet	12½"	6¼"

All of the shots fired by a competitor on his own target will make a group on the backing card which will be an exact duplicate of his group on the record target. But should a shooter at the firing point to the right of the competitor fire a shot on the competitor's target, the bullet hole made by that shot in the backing card will be 1/4 inch to the left of its corresponding hole in the record target, and shots fired from the second firing point to the right would be 1/2 inch to the left on the backing card, etc. Thus the shots from the shooters on either side can be eliminated from the competitor's target, and the competitor given full value for all the shots he has fired on his target. Also the shooters who fired on the wrong target can be identified and penalized. To make this system work each competitor must fire with his rifle close to his number stake at his firing point.

The double target rack, one for each competitor, is usually set up permanently at the butt, the upright supports being planted in the ground. A range assistant takes the record targets and backing cards of a relay down to the racks, the signal "Cease Firing" having previously been given. The assistant takes out the record targets and backing cards of the previous relay (taking care to keep each backing card behind its record target) and then fastens the record targets and backing cards of the new relay in their proper place. Each record target and backing card is numbered with the number of the firing point and the number of the relay.

It is best, where sufficient land is available, to have separate butts and separate firing points for the various distances to be used, but it is possible to get along with a butt at 100 yards only, and between the firing point and the butt to place posts only on which the racks of targets for either 50 feet or 50 yards can be hung. In fact, the fence is not absolutely necessary at the butt, but it costs little or nothing, as it can be made of scrap materials, and it makes the targets stand out plain and distinct, and gives something on which to place the large numbers designating which target belongs to which firing point.

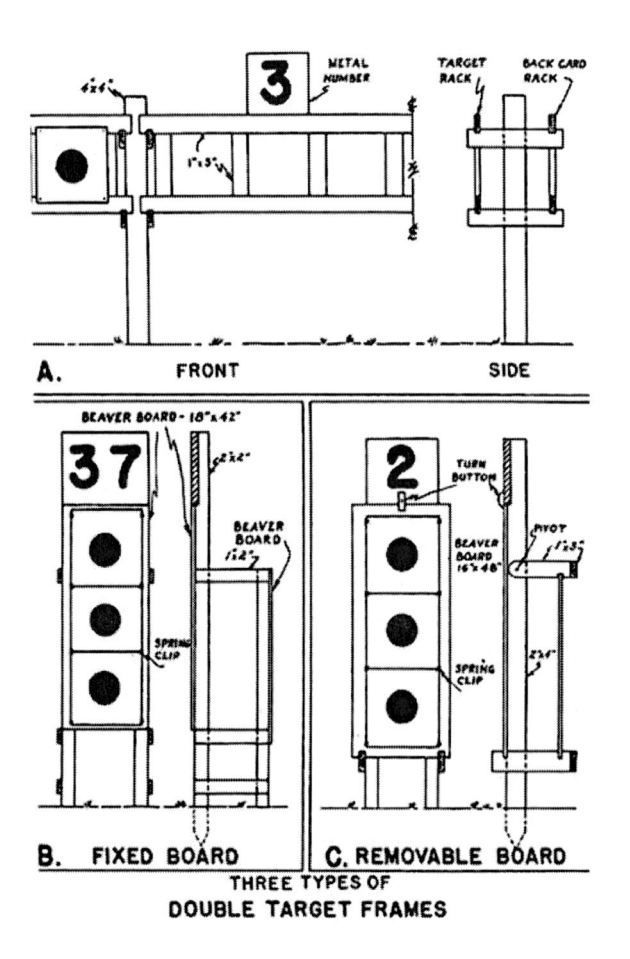

PLATE 34

The firing point ought to be raised a little above the surrounding ground, both to keep it dry and enable view to be had of the targets when firing prone without having to cut the grass so often. The mound ought to be at least 7 feet from the front to rear on top, and should slope very slightly to the rear. At the front of each individual firing point there should be a stake with a number painted on it corresponding to the number painted on the butt above the corresponding target position. There should be at least five, preferably six, feet between each individual firing point. It adds to the convenience and comfort if a simple roof can be erected over the firing point. This roof should be about 8 feet from front to rear and should slope about a foot toward the front, being 6 1/2 to 7 feet high in the clear at the rear. It can be made of scrap lumber covered with tar paper. The shooter takes his position or lies down just behind the stake bearing his number, and fires on the target or targets at the butt corresponding to the number of his stake. In order to see where each bullet strikes his target, he must be provided with a spotting telescope which he sets up on a holder to one side, so that, by moving his head slightly to one side when in firing position, he can view his target through the glass and see the bullet holes. This and the cheap construction cost are the great advantages of the short distance small bore outdoor ranges. No hired markers are necessary, the telescopes taking their places.

All of the above is not necessary where only two or three shooters wish to fire together. The writer and a few of his friends have gotten along very well for years with nothing more elaborate than a measured range in a field, and a large packing box filled with earth for a butt, on the front of which the targets were tacked. But all of those who used this range were good and careful shots and they kept all their bullets on the box.

200-YARD BUTTS

If an individual or club wishes to shoot at 200 yards and has that distance available on the outdoor range, a little more elaborate butt and target carrier is necessary. It is only in the most perfect light, and when no mirage or heat waves are present, that the best spotting telescopes will show .22 caliber bullet holes at 200 yards. Therefore when shooting at this range it is necessary to have a man or boy as a marker at the butt to indicate the value and location of each shot on the target. The butt must be so constructed that it will shelter the marker from any possibility of being struck by a bullet. This butt may be a box-like shelter about three feet thick filled with earth, or it may be a pit in the ground, or a combination of the two. The targets are fastened to frames, which are best made about four feet square, covered with cotton cloth over which heavy paper has been pasted, the targets being pinned in the center of the frame. The larger paper backing shows most of the shots which miss the target and this is quite desirable, as the C-5 target is not very high vertically and many shots miss it and are hard to locate. These frames are arranged on sliding carriers so that they slide behind the butt where the marker puts in the spotter and pastes the old bullet hole and then slides into firing position, either above or to one side of the butt.

A backstop to catch the bullets is, of course, very necessary, and if this is not provided by a hill or other obstacle, a large one must be built, box-like, and filled with earth or gravel.

Plate 35 shows the construction of a simple type of 200-yard small bore butt, comprising a target house, marker's shelter, target carriers, and artificial backstop, that is relatively simple and inexpensive to build and yet answers every purpose. It permits four shooters to fire at one time, there being two targets at each side of the shelter. All boxes shown are filled to the top with sand or fine gravel. The markers are fully protected by the box connected to the house and by chicken wire fastened securely over both ends of the house so that no part of the body can be exposed or be directly in the line of fire. The artificial backstops behind the targets are necessary only when there is no natural bullet stop. The boxes will, of course, gradually get shot away immediately behind the targets, and to avoid having to repair them constantly that portion of the backstop immediately behind the targets where ninety per cent of the bullets strike may be covered with a steel plate set at an angle of 45 degrees to deflect the bullets downward, or railroad ties or logs may be piled up.

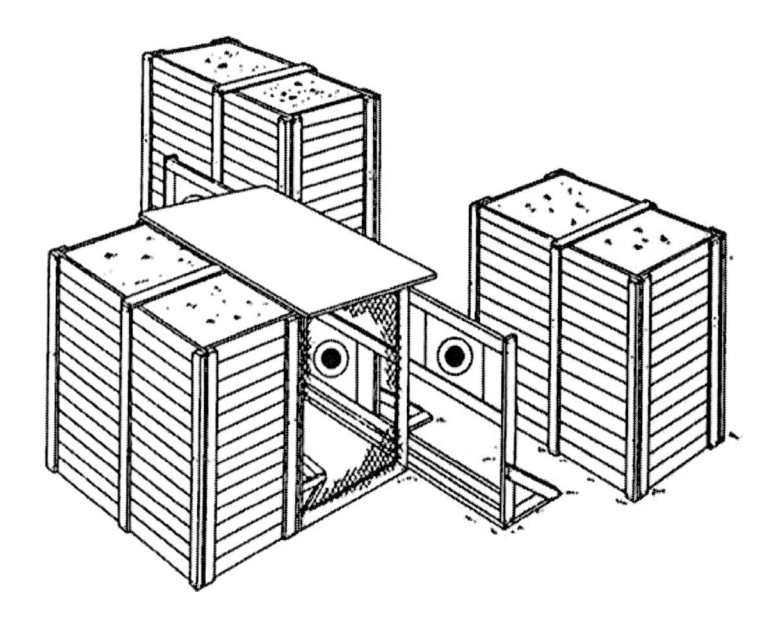

PLATE 35—Home-Made 200-Yard Butt and Target Carrier

The target frames are arranged to slide as shown in a wooden framework. The marker slides the frame out into the exposed position. When it is fired on he pulls it into the shelter, places a target spotter in the new bullet hole, pastes up the old bullet hole with a paster, and slides the target into position again for another shot. The spotters are 2-inch-round cardboard discs, white on one side (for hits in the bull's-eye) and black on the other, with a wire or .22-inch peg stuck through them and projecting to each side. This spotter, stuck through the last bullet hole, is visible from the firing point through the shooter's spotting telescope, and shows him exactly where his last shot struck. For shots in the bull's-eye the spotter is stuck through the bullet hole with the white side showing and can be seen easily through the telescope.

Markers must be very careful how they leave the shelter at such a butt. The targets must first be withdrawn, and a red flag displayed in their place.

Instead of having the targets arranged to slide out at each side of a short shelter as shown, the shelter may be made continuous as in a large military rifle range, and the carriers built so that the target frames will slide vertically to an exposed position above the shelter. This is the best arrangement where there are to be more than four shooters firing at the same time. Or, if desired, a regular military target carrier may be used, the standard small bore target being pinned on the frame in lieu of the regular military target.

SAFETY REGULATIONS

On any rifle range the following safety regulations must be strictly enforced. Anyone who disregards these regulations should be subject to dismissal from the range.

1. A rifle must never under any circumstances be pointed at or in the direction of any person, whether it be loaded or not.

2. All rifles must habitually be carried with the breech

action open until the shooter take his place at the firing point with the rifle pointed in the direction of the target.

3. No rifle shall be loaded unless the shooter is in position at the firing point with the rifle pointed at the target, and then not until the range officer shall have given the command "Commence Firing", or "Load".

4. At the command "Cease Firing" or when a shooter is through firing he shall at once unload his rifle, and lay it down, muzzle to the front, breech open.

5. On ranges where it is necessary for a person to walk out in front of the firing point to change targets, no person shall do so without permission of the range officer who shall first command "Cease Firing" and then watch to see that all shooters have unloaded and laid down their rifles. On gallery ranges the target lights shall also be turned off.

6. When there are markers at the butt, the markers shall not leave their shelter nor expose themselves until they have withdrawn all targets from the firing position, have exposed the red danger flags and have received the signal that all is safe from the firing point. In the absence of a telephone connecting butts and firing point, this "All Clear" signal may be given by horn or bugle.

For further information relative to rifle ranges, write to The Secretary, National Rifle Association, 1600 Rhode Island Ave., Washington, D. C., stating the information desired.

CHAPTER XIV

THE RIFLE CLUB AND THE NATIONAL RIFLE ASSOCIATION

In any community where a number of individuals are interested in rifle or pistol shooting it is to the advantage of all of them to organize a rifle and pistol club. Such a club helps each shooter by introducing the element of competition and sport, which adds considerably to the enjoyment of any pastime by establishing contact with other shooters and providing for an exchange of ideas and experiments and by enlisting the interest of the community at large through the medium of the rifle and pistol matches which the club can hold and the resulting newspaper publicity. There is the further consideration that the construction of a range by an individual is frequently out of the question, due to the cost, but, where a group of men get together into a club and pool their funds through initiation fees and club dues, the matter of acquiring a range becomes comparatively simple.

While a club may be loosely organized among a group of congenial spirits, it is far better to have the group properly organized along the officially recognized lines and to affiliate the local club with the National Rifle Association of America. Clubs so organized and affiliated enjoy numerous advantages, among which may be mentioned the holding of a nationally recognized charter; the privilege of qualifying for the Regular Army marksmanship decorations—Marksman, Sharpshooter and Expert Rifleman and Marksman, Sharpshooter and Expert Pistol Shot; the privilege of competing in nation-wide interclub matches sanctioned by the National Rifle Association; the privilege of purchasing ammunition, paper targets, spare parts for rifles, etc., direct from the War Department; the receipt of programs, bulletins and other publications issued by the National Rifle Association, including "The American Rifleman" each month. Up until June 30, 1927, civilian rifle clubs were entitled to draw under bond from the War Department a limited number of rifles, some ammunition, targets and target carriers and similar supplies without cost to themselves. The economy program of the administration induced Congress, however, to appropriate only enough money to continue this aid to clubs already in existence and did not provide for assistance to newly organized clubs. For this reason, rifle clubs now organizing cannot obtain assistance from the War Department without cost to themselves, but they may, if they so desire, place a requisition on file with the Director of Civilian Marksmanship to be filled when supplies again become available.

The affiliation of a rifle and pistol club with the National

Rifle Association requires a minimum of ten citizens of the United States, sixteen years of age or older for a senior club, or not over nineteen years of age for a junior club. Clubs may be organized in schools, colleges, fraternal organizations, industrial plants, athletic clubs, fish and game protective associations, or just among groups of interested citizens who have no other affiliations. At least ten men must pay their initiation fees and dues into the club before it can be recognized by the National Rifle Association. There is no maximum, however, to the number of men who may be enrolled under one club charter. The club dues are not fixed by the National Rifle Association, but may be placed at any figure which is deemed advisable by the club itself. A senior club pays ten dollars per year dues, while junior and college clubs pay five dollars per year dues to the National Rifle Association. This fee is the same, regardless of how many members there are in the club.

The necessary application blanks and more detailed information may be obtained by writing to the National Rifle Association, 1600 Rhode Island Ave., Washington, D. C. It is required that application for club affiliations be made on the regular application blanks which are furnished by the Association.

There are at the present time about three thousand rifle and pistol clubs in the United States operating under National Rifle Association charters, so that there is ample opportunity for the local club to arrange a wide variety of matches with other organizations, in addition to the local matches which should be arranged between club members and the National Matches under the sanction of the National Rifle Association.

INDIVIDUAL N. R. A. MEMBERSHIP

In order that a satisfactory check-up may be made and a record kept of arms sold by the War Department, it is required that an individual be an individual member of the National Rifle Association, rather than a club member, before he can purchase a rifle or revolver. These individual members are required to be indorsed by someone who is already a member of the Association or by some of their local police or National Guard authorities.

There are several types of individual membership open to men who desire to support the rifle and pistol shooting game without being members of clubs, or in addition to their club membership. The two most popular types of individual membership are known as Annual Membership, which as the name implies, is a membership for twelve months, and Life Membership, which gives the holder the privileges of membership for life. Annual membership costs three dollars per year, and life membership fifty dollars. These individual members may, under normal conditions, buy military arms and ammunition direct from the War Department; they may compete in the numerous Individual Matches which are conducted by the Association throughout the year; they receive

"The American Rifleman" magazine regularly every month; they receive direct all programs, bulletins and other materials gotten out by National Headquarters; they are entitled to the personal advice and suggestions of the experts retained by the National Rifle Association to advise its members in regard to their shooting problems; and they, of course, receive the golden bronze membership button and the membership card of the Association. In addition to these general privileges, Life Members have the privilege of voting at the Annual Election of Directors of the Association and they may occupy Directors' Chairs and be elected to the Executive Committee of the Association.

"THE AMERICAN RIFLEMAN"

"The American Rifleman" magazine which has been frequently mentioned in this chapter is the official publication of the National Rifle Association. It is the only magazine published in America devoted exclusively to shooting subjects. Among the shooters who have known this magazine for years you will find the general impression prevailing that if "The American Rifleman" says so, it is so. Among other unique features of this shooters' magazine may be mentioned the fact that it maintains a "Question and Answer Department" in charge of a nationally recognized expert in the technique of arms, ammunition, and rifle and pistol shooting who will solve as far as possible by mail the problems which confront members.

"The American Rifleman" is sent to all club secretaries without charge and to all life members and annual members without additional charge. Club members may subscribe for the magazine through their club secretaries at the price of one dollar and a half per year. The regular subscription price for the publication is three dollars per year.